Jokerman

Reading the Lyrics of
Bob Dylan

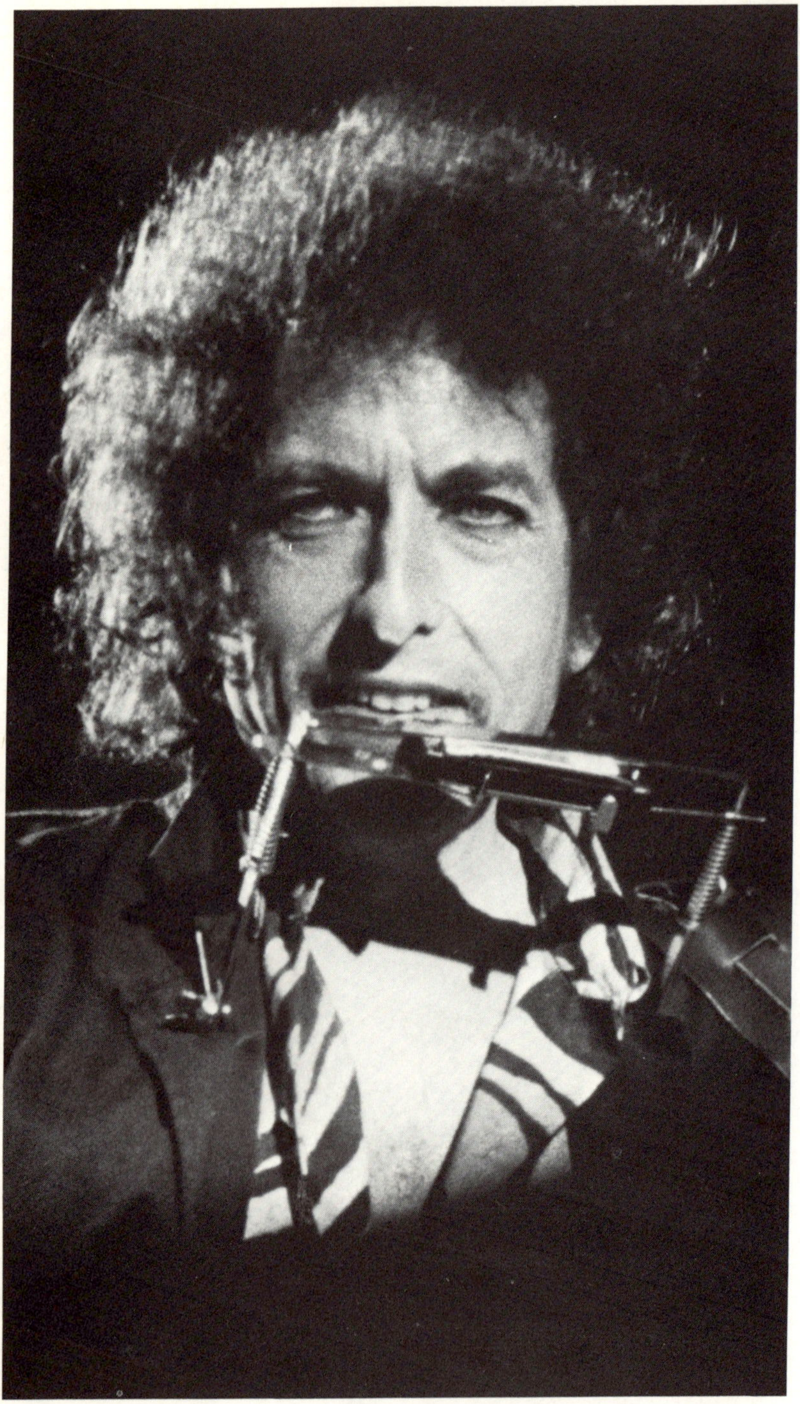

Jokerman

Reading the Lyrics of Bob Dylan

Aidan Day

Basil Blackwell

Copyright © Aidan Day 1988

First published 1988

First published in paperback 1989

Basil Blackwell Ltd
108 Cowley Road, Oxford, OX4 1JF, UK

Basil Blackwell, Inc.
3 Cambridge Center
Cambridge, Massachusetts 02142, USA

All rights reserved. Except for the quotation of short passages for the purposes of criticism and review, no part of this publication may be reproduced, stored in a retrieval system, or transmitted, in any form or by any means, electronic, mechanical, photocopying, recording or otherwise, without the prior permission of the publisher.

Except in the United States of America, this book is sold subject to the condition that it shall not, by way of trade or otherwise, be lent, re-sold, hired out, or otherwise circulated without the publisher's prior consent in any form of binding or cover other than that in which it is published and without a similar condition including this condition being imposed on the subsequent purchaser.

British Library Cataloguing in Publication Data

Day, Aidan
  Jokerman: reading the lyrics of Bob Dylan
  1. Pop songs in English. American writers.
  Dylan, Bob. Words – Critical studies
  I. Title
  784.5′0092′4
  ISBN 0-631-15873-1
  ISBN 0-631-17245-9 (pbk)

Library of Congress Cataloging in Publication Data

Day, Aidan.
  Jokerman: reading the lyrics of Bob Dylan.
  Bibliography: p.
  Includes index.
  1. Dylan, Bob, 1941–   – Criticism and interpretation.
  I. Title.
  PS3554.Y56Z634   1988   811′.54   88-6104
  ISBN 0-631-15873-1
  ISBN 0-631-17245-9 (pbk.)

Typeset in 13 on 15pt Bembo
by Joshua Associates Ltd., Oxford
Printed in Great Britain
by T. J. Press Ltd., Padstow

'harlequin words, harlequin language'
H.D., *Her*

To Sandra Kemp

Contents

Note on this Edition		viii
Acknowledgements		ix
Textual Note		xiii

1 **Words** — 1

2 **Mouths** — 8
'Ballad of a Thin Man' (1965)

3 **Reels of Rhyme** — 19
'Mr. Tambourine Man' (1965); 'Eternal Circle' (1963); 'Love Minus Zero/No Limit' (1965)

4 **Lady Language Creator** — 36
'Isis' (1976); 'I Shall Be Released' (1967); 'Tangled Up in Blue' (1975); 'Shelter from the Storm' (1975)

5 **That Enemy Within** — 71
'Brownsville Girl' (1986); 'It's All Over Now, Baby Blue' (1965); 'Desolation Row' (1965); 'She Belongs to Me' (1965); 'New Pony' (1978)

Contents

6 To Separate the Good from the Bad   96
Christian lyrics (1979, 1981); 'Precious Angel' (1979); 'Heart of Mine' (1981)

7 That Forbidden Zone   110
'Visions of Johanna' (1966); 'I and I' (1983); 'All Along the Watchtower' (1968); 'Jokerman' (1983)

Appendix   Chronology of Dylan's Career and Officially Released Recordings   145

Notes   180

Index   187

Note on this Edition

In this paperback edition a passage in Chapter 1 has been recast, some factual errors have been corrected and the Chronology has been brought up to date.

Acknowledgements

For help that cannot be summarized, I am deeply indebted to Christopher Ricks, Kathryn Burlinson, Alison Stewart and Taeran Dypneen. I should warmly like to thank my editor at Basil Blackwell, John Davey. My thanks also to Chris McKay for compiling the index.

For permission to quote from lyrics written by Bob Dylan, I am very grateful to the undermentioned copyright holders:

'Abandoned Love' Copyright © 1975, 1976 Ram's Horn Music. Used by permission. All rights reserved.
'All Along the Watchtower' Copyright © 1968 Dwarf Music. Used by permission. All rights reserved.
'Ballad of a Thin Man' Copyright © 1965 Warner Bros. Inc. Used by permission. All rights reserved.
'Blowin' in the Wind' Copyright © 1962 Warner Bros. Inc. Used by permission. All rights reserved.
'Brownsville Girl' [words co-written with Sam Shepard] Copyright © 1986. Special Rider Music. Used by permission. All rights reserved.
'Caribbean Wind' Copyright © 1985 Special Rider Music. Used by permission. All rights reserved.
'Changing of the Guards' Copyright © 1978 Special Rider Music. Used by permission. All rights reserved.
'Dead Man, Dead Man' Copyright © 1981 Special Rider Music. Used by permission. All rights reserved.
'Desolation Row' Copyright © 1965 Warner Bros. Inc. Used by permission. All rights reserved.

Acknowledgements

'11 Outlined Epitaphs' Copyright © 1964 Special Rider Music. Used by permission. All rights reserved.

'Eternal Circle' Copyright © 1963, 1964 Warner Bros. Inc. Used by permission. All rights reserved.

'Every Grain of Sand' Copyright © 1981 Special Rider Music. Used by permission. All rights reserved.

'Golden Loom' Copyright © 1975, 1976 Ram's Horn Music. Used by permission. All rights reserved.

'Gonna Change My Way of Thinking' Copyright © 1979 Special Rider Music. Used by permission. All rights reserved.

'Gotta Serve Somebody' Copyright © 1979 Special Rider Music. Used by permission. All rights reserved.

'A Hard Rain's A-Gonna Fall' Copyright © 1963 Warner Bros. Inc. Used by permission. All rights reserved.

'Heart of Mine' Copyright © 1981 Special Rider Music. Used by permission. All rights reserved.

'I and I' Copyright © 1983 Special Rider Music. Used by permission. All rights reserved.

'I Shall Be Free No. 10' Copyright © 1971, 1973 Special Rider Music. Used by permission. All rights reserved.

'I Shall Be Released' Copyright © 1967, 1970 Dwarf Music. Used by permission. All rights reserved.

'Isis' [words co-written with Jacques Levy] Copyright © 1975, 1976 Ram's Horn Music. Used by permission. All rights reserved.

'It's All Over Now, Baby Blue' Copyright © 1965 Warner Bros. Inc. Used by permission. All rights reserved.

'I Wanna Be Your Lover' Copyright © 1971, 1976 Dwarf Music. Used by permission. All rights reserved.

'Jokerman' Copyright © 1983 Special Rider Music. Used by permission. All rights reserved.

'Lenny Bruce' Copyright © 1981 Special Rider Music. Used by permission. All rights reserved.

'Like a Rolling Stone' Copyright © 1965 Warner Bros. Inc. Used by permission. All rights reserved.

'Love Minus Zero/No Limit' Copyright © 1965 Warner Bros. Inc. Used by permission. All rights reserved.

'Man of Peace' Copyright © 1983 Special Rider Music. Used by permission. All rights reserved.

Acknowledgements

'Mr. Tambourine Man' Copyright © 1964, 1965 Warner Bros. Inc. Used by permission. All rights reserved.

'My Back Pages' Copyright © 1964 Warner Bros. Inc. Used by permission. All rights reserved.

'New Pony' Copyright © 1978 Special Rider Music. Used by permission. All rights reserved.

'Obviously Five Believers' Copyright © 1966 Dwarf Music. Used by permission. All rights reserved.

'Oh, Sister' Copyright © 1975, 1976 Ram's Horn Music. Used by permission. All rights reserved.

'One of Us Must Know (Sooner or Later)' Copyright © 1966 Dwarf Music. Used by permission. All rights reserved.

'Precious Angel' Copyright © 1979 Special Rider Music. Used by permission. All rights reserved.

'Property of Jesus' Copyright © 1981 Special Rider Music. Used by permission. All rights reserved.

'Señor (Tales of Yankee Power)' Copyright © 1978 Special Rider Music. Used by permission. All rights reserved.

'She Belongs to Me' Copyright © 1965 Warner Bros. Inc. Used by permission. All rights reserved.

'Shelter from the Storm' Copyright © 1974, 1975 Ram's Horn Music. Used by permission. All rights reserved.

'She's Your Lover Now' Copyright © 1971, 1976 Dwarf Music. Used by permission. All rights reserved.

'Shot of Love' Copyright © 1981 Special Rider Music. Used by permission. All rights reserved.

'Slow Train' Copyright © 1979 Special Rider Music. Used by permission. All rights reserved.

'Song to Woody' Copyright © 1962, 1965 Duchess Music Corporation. Used by permission. All rights reserved.

'Stuck Inside of Mobile with the Memphis Blues Again' Copyright © 1966 Dwarf Music. Used by permission. All rights reserved.

'Subterranean Homesick Blues' Copyright © 1965 Warner Bros. Inc. Used by permission. All rights reserved.

'Tangled Up in Blue' Copyright © 1974, 1975 Ram's Horn Music. Used by permission. All rights reserved.

'Temporary Like Achilles' Copyright © 1966 Dwarf Music. Used by permission. All rights reserved.

Acknowledgements

'Tombstone Blues' Copyright © 1965 Warner Bros. Inc. Used by permission. All rights reserved.

'Trouble' Copyright © 1981 Special Rider Music. Used by permission. All rights reserved.

'Trouble in Mind' Copyright © 1979 Special Rider Music. Used by permission. All rights reserved.

'Visions of Johanna' Copyright © 1966 Dwarf Music. Used by permission. All rights reserved.

'Watered-Down Love' Copyright © 1981 Special Rider Music. Used by permission. All rights reserved.

'When He Returns' Copyright © 1979 Special Rider Music. Used by permission. All rights reserved.

'When You Gonna Wake Up?' Copyright © 1979 Special Rider Music. Used by permission. All rights reserved.

'Where Are You Tonight? (Journey Through Dark Heat)' Copyright © 1978 Special Rider Music. Used by permission. All rights reserved.

'You're Gonna Make Me Lonesome When You Go' Copyright © 1974, 1975 Ram's Horn Music. Used by permission. All rights reserved.

Frontispiece: Dylan in concert at Newcastle, England, 1984; reproduced by courtesy of Tony Kenwright.

Textual Note

Except where noted otherwise, the texts of Dylan's words are taken from *Bob Dylan: Lyrics, 1962-1985* (Knopf, 1985; Cape, 1987). The record album on which a performance of a lyric originally appeared is given on first citation of the lyric. The records from which I have principally drawn my examples of Dylan lyrics are sometimes referred to using the abbreviations listed below. Performances of certain lyrics have been released only on retrospective records. In such cases the date of the first known recording accompanies reference to the latest retrospective record on which a performance of the lyric appears. Where a performance of a lyric has never officially been released, only the date of the first known recording is given. Information on recording dates is drawn mainly from Michael Krogsgaard, *Master of the Tracks: The Bob Dylan Reference Book of Recording* (Scandinavian Institute for Rock-Research, 1988).

Officially Released Dylan Record Albums, 1962–1989 and List of Abbreviated References

      Bob Dylan (1962)
      The Freewheelin' Bob Dylan (1963)
      The Times They Are A-Changin' (1964)
      Another Side of Bob Dylan (1964)
BABH *Bringing It All Back Home* (1965)

Textual Note

H61	*Highway 61 Revisited* (1965)
BB	*Blonde on Blonde* (1966)
	Bob Dylan's Greatest Hits [Retrospective Collection] (1967)
JWH	*John Wesley Harding* (1968)
	Nashville Skyline (1969)
	Self Portrait (1970)
	New Morning (1970)
	Bob Dylan's Greatest Hits, Vol. 2 [Retrospective Collection] (1971)
	Pat Garrett & Billy the Kid [Film Soundtrack] (1973)
	Dylan [Studio Outtakes, 1969-70] (1973)
	Planet Waves (1974)
	Before the Flood [Concert Performances] (1974)
BT	*Blood on the Tracks* (1975)
	The Basement Tapes [Private Recording Sessions, 1967] (1975)
D	*Desire* (1976)
	Hard Rain [Concert Performances] (1976)
	Bob Dylan: Masterpieces [Retrospective Collection] (1978)
SL	*Street Legal* (1978)
	Bob Dylan at Budokan [Concert Performances] (1978)
STC	*Slow Train Coming* (1979)
	Saved (1980)
SOL	*Shot of Love* (1981)
I	*Infidels* (1983)
	Real Live [Concert Performances] (1984)
	Empire Burlesque (1985)
	Biograph [Retrospective Collection] (1985)
	Knocked Out Loaded (1986)
	Down in the Groove (1988)
	Dylan and the Dead [Concert Performances] (1989)

1
Words

I and I
In creation where one's nature neither honors nor forgives.
I and I
One says to the other, no man sees my face and lives.
'I and I', *Infidels*

'It *is* mostly about identity.' Dylan's comment on his 1978 film *Renaldo and Clara* may be applied to the collection of verse which he has produced since 1962.[1] The issue of identity constitutes a primary imaginative focus of that body of work. It is the specific preoccupation of a large proportion of the lyrics and it recurs as a consideration throughout the wide range of distinguishable subjects that are canvassed in the verse. The present book concentrates on providing close readings of individual lyrics selected principally from that side of Dylan's lyrical writing which takes up questions of identity. The study does not attempt to survey the entirety of Dylan's verse output, amounting to some several hundred lyrics, nor does it directly address other major areas of concern in his work, such as social and political commentary or love (although, in the latter case, there is at times significant interchange between the representation of lovers' attitudes and relationships and the figuring of individual identity). The lyrics discussed are chosen from throughout his writing career, the latest having been released on record in 1986.

Matters of identity are not, in this study, biographical matters. This book does not concern itself with the 'life'. The 'I and I' of the epigraph is symptomatic of the many divisions of the self offered in Dylan's art – not least the ceaseless transformations of persona in his stage appearances – that would mock any attempt to contain his art through reference to biographical events.

Biography apart, Dylan's lyrics resist containment within the roles often assigned to words, voice and music. 'Cawing, derisive' was Philip Larkin's account of Dylan's voice on the 1965 album *Highway 61 Revisited*.[2] It would be possible – taking his career as a whole – to distinguish an extraordinary variety of Dylan voices, not all of which would be captured by Larkin's description here. But Larkin's adjectives are not only an excellent register of the *Highway 61* voice, they also suggest something of the peculiar tonal quality common to nearly all of Dylan's performances. Typically, the voice engages the line of the melody but its simultaneously jarring, atonal separation from the music, together with the relentless subordination of musical elements to the exigencies of verbal order, opens a space which registers a distance and an unease involving both singer and listener. The singing voice at once solicits and rebuffs. The gratifications it offers are uncomfortable ones. It is a pattern of invitation and rejection in which the audience – alienated from easy absorption into the music and denied relaxation – is required to attend closely to the transactions between voice and words. While the voice impinges distinctively on the listener, it simultaneously seeks to refuse an unthinking capitulation to itself and to the sense of what it is singing. It is a pattern which places special demands upon an audience, expecting it to participate actively – and to risk itself – in the play of meaning.

But the most important resistance in Dylan's lyrics is to the

Words

role now commonly ascribed to words written for singing. Ezra Pound observed that the Provençals or troubadours triumphed 'in an art between literature and music' and that the Elizabethans also achieved 'a poetry that could be sung'.[3] But in the modern period the composition of such a poetry is, as Pound put it, 'wellnigh a lost art',[4] and there is a popular modern sense that the verbal semantics of a song will necessarily be less rich, the lexical textures less deeply conceived, than those of poetry; that music, to use Pound's terms, 'turns . . . words out of doors and strews them and distorts them to the tune, out of all recognition' as poetry.[5] There are some slight enough verbal pieces within Dylan's prolific output. Such pieces often, in performance, work simply and powerfully as songs. The distinctiveness of Dylan's achievement, however, is the very large extent to which his lyrics transgress any ready distinction between a poetic richness of signification, a density of verbal meaning, on the one hand, and performance as song, on the other.

Yet there are many different kinds of richness in Dylan's lyrical writing. There are types of Dylan lyric that – for all their formal sculptings, for all their verbal subtleties and intensities – present no special structural, syntactic, or imagistic problems. But there are many lyrics which manifest exactly such problems, lyrics which characteristically display a difficulty and an opacity, a dislocation of common sense. Concentrating on Dylan's explorations of identity, this study inevitably concentrates on lyrics defined by such obscurities in structure and verbal texture. Not all Dylan's lyrics dealing with identity fall simply into this category and not all lyrics in this category are necessarily concerned immediately with identity. There is, however, an important correlation between the category and the subject of identity.

It is in these lyrics which display disruptions – to varying degrees and in various kinds – of rational order and logical

3

sequence that Dylan's work reveals a cardinal inheritance from the practices of classic modernist poetry. Frank Kermode, commenting on Dylan's first radical shift in the mid-1960s from his earliest political manner into forms of poetic obscurity ('protest offered too simple a kind of authenticity' and the songs of the mid-1960s 'have to do with a more complex notion of truth'), has observed that Dylan

> remains a poet, as he has remained a virtuoso of the voice – snarling, pushing words and tunes askew, endlessly inventive.... What he offers is mystery, not just opacity.... His poems have to be open... inviting collusion. To write thus is to practice a very modern art, though, as Dylan is well aware, it is an art with a complicated past.[6]

One of the complications of Dylan's aesthetic modernity is the demotic openness of his use of language. Dylan's lyrics embrace a mixture of registers without granting any special authority to poetic voices that eschew the colloquial. The intermingling of 'literary' and non-literary language in Dylan's work knows no hierarchies of evaluation and restraint. Neither studiously avoiding nor ingratiating themselves with either the vernacular or the literary his lyrics refuse a divide between the popular and the literary. Dylan's ...in' endings unforcedly exchange with his ...ings ('Someone else is speakin' with my mouth, but I'm listening only to my heart'); usage modulates freely with usage ('Ain't it just like the night...' but 'is our purpose not the same on this earth'). Comparably, as Christopher Ricks has argued, Dylan's lyrics do not get 'proudly trapped in the illusion that you can free yourself from clichés by having no truck with them'[7]:

> Bob Dylan's art does not traffic in clichés, but it travels far and near by the vehicle of cliché.... Dylan has a newly instinctive grasp of the age-old instincts which created a cliché in the first place, and this is manifest on all the occasions when he throws new light on an old cliché, or rotates a cliché so that a facet of it catches a new light....[8]

Words

The simultaneous familiarity and originality of revisioned clichés in Dylan find a parallel in the uses to which refrains are put in his verse. The difficulty of a Dylan lyric may lie not merely in an indirectness of language in the stanzas, but in a density of allusion and pun. Yet where there is such difficulty it is habitually offset by an affirmation of shared involvement in the repetition of a phrase – often itself a cliché – in refrain; while such a phrase will at the same time stand adjusted in an individual light through its relationship with the words of the stanzas.

It does not fall within the scope of this study to comment extensively on features of the performance of the lyrics. Nor does it set out to analyse the way in which elements of the prosody of Dylan's lyrics differ – in the framing of that prosody to sung performance – from certain conventions belonging to the tradition of English accentual-syllabic verse. The semantic properties of the words of the lyrics are the primary interest of the study and it offers speculative readings of the lyric texts as printed without musical setting in the lyric book prepared by Dylan. This is not to claim priority for the printed text over the performance, nor to undervalue the profound expressive possibilities of Dylan's voice. A Dylan lyric on the page is one text of that lyric while a performance of it constitutes another. Nor is there necessarily one dominant performed version. A live interpretation of a song may stand equally with its performance on a studio-album and so on. What we have in Dylan's art is a complex variety of possible texts. Concentration on printed versions of Dylan's lyrics excludes consideration of the expanded expressive range belonging to performances of those lyrics. Nevertheless, the words alone stand as significant texts, soliciting study in their own right much as (though the analogy is not exact) the words of a play may invite study in isolation from performance.

The book does not propose a simple linear development in Dylan's lyrical exploration of questions of identity. Alterations in diction and linguistic resource or modifications in conceptual and imaginative terms of reference are, of course, discernible at various points in his career. But, these tend to be experimental shifts of emphasis or creative adjustments in angles of approach to certain constant themes and concerns rather than radical breaks or traumatic new departures. In their treatments of identity the lyrics do not move in a single line of progression, but throughout Dylan's career gather in orbits around a number of recurrent preoccupations. Thus while the study opens with a discussion of works from 1965 and ends by considering lyrics from 1983, this does not indicate the adoption of a strict chronological sequence and there are points where lyrics written many years apart will be juxtaposed for discussion within a particular thematic grouping.

The following chapter provides an introductory examination of the challenge put in Dylan's work to a conception of the self as a single or monolithic entity. It offers a preliminary discussion of Dylan's treatment, above all, of energies of the psyche which lie outside the limits and control of the rational self.

Such energies are associated in certain Dylan lyrics with the mind's imaginative capacities and, in particular, with the sources of artistic creation. Chapter 3 goes on to consider examples of lyrics which make this association and which, in considering the grounds of artistic creation, conduct a self-reflexive inquiry into their own origins.

Dylan's lyrics which focus on the nature and processes of poetic creation characteristically dramatize a tension between inspiration and form, between unconscious or imaginative resources and the linguistic articulation of those resources. A parallel drama is to be found in those of Dylan's lyrics which, opening out into an exploration of the broad dynamics of the psyche, read in it a discontinuity between conscious and unconscious dimensions of the mind. The fourth chapter concentrates upon lyrics that offer a vision of identity as locked in tension between, on the one hand, the conscious, socialized self that has its being in language, and on the other, those drives of personality that exceed rational formulation and social definition.

The fifth chapter considers further Dylan's preoccupation with the senses in which the conscious, linguistically defined self may be fixed in culturally preformulated roles. It also extends discussion of Dylan's lyric celebration of the compulsion of irrational forces towards a transformation of such fixture. But while many Dylan lyrics are passionately concerned with the positive and redemptive potential of areas of identity outside reason and language, this chapter goes on to examine an equivalent engagement in his work with a dark, negative potential in these areas.

Conviction of the existence of powers which – for good or ill – override management by the conscious personality sets the terms of Dylan's explicitly Christian lyrics. Chapter 6 examines the striving towards an absolute separation of dark and light forces in mind and world which typifies Dylan's Christian lyrics. It discusses both the successes of those lyrics in discriminating the positive from the negative, the graceful from the malign, and the way in which they at the same time persistently undermine their own discriminations.

The self-undermining possibilities of the Christian lyrics point beyond those lyrics to works by Dylan that emphasize neither dark nor light powers, nor even a contrast or conflict between these, but an interpenetration of creative and destructive energies within the mind and in reality. Dylan continually returns to contemplation of this confusion and the final chapter considers examples of lyrics whose framing of the multiform and bizarre energies of identity constitutes Dylan's most distinctive achievement.

2

Mouths

> light of feelin'
> as I listen t'one of my own tongues
> take the reins
> guide the path
> an' drop me off...
>   '11 Outlined Epitaphs' (1964)[1]

'I cannot say the word eye any more' wrote Dylan in the 1965 album notes to *Highway 61 Revisited*. The observation forms part of a prose passage which, punning on the homophone I/eye, playfully hints at a scepticism regarding the attribution of a fixed meaning to the term 'I'. It is a scepticism elaborated in the passage as Dylan explores a self that is divided – observing itself as it might observe another – by virtue of its very self-consciousness. In place of the single reality conventionally identified by the first-person pronoun the passage substitutes an image of 'mouths' of the self. Such a plurality of mouths, tongues or voices, calls into question the monolithic authority of the conscious 'I' that is associated with the upper reaches (the 'rooftop') of the mind:

I cannot say the word eye any more.... when I speak this word eye, it is as if I am speaking of somebody's eye that I faintly remember.... there is no I – there is only a series of mouths – long live the mouths – your rooftop – if you don't already know – has been demolished. . . .[2]

The preoccupation with questions of identity, and the punning, carry over into the lyrics of *Highway 61 Revisited*. 'Like a Rolling Stone', for example, inquires into the disquiet of living unprotected by the learned values of established culture. 'You've gone to the finest school alright, Miss Lonely', but 'nobody has ever taught you how to live on the street':

> How does it feel
> To be without a home . . .?

And how does it feel to be without the reassurance of accepted ways of thinking about the self? Living on the street is in this lyric expressly a matter of living without a rooftop. The rhyme pattern in the second stanza recalls the sleeve-note pun on I/eye:

> You said you'd never compromise
> With the mystery tramp, but now you realize
> He's not selling any alibis
> As you stare into the vacuum of his eyes

It is within an interior cityscape that the denizen of the streets, the 'mystery tramp', is encountered. Looking forward to the figure of the joker in Dylan's 1983 'Jokerman' (*Infidels*), the 'mystery tramp' images possibilities of the psyche not contained solely within the field of the conscious or rational self. Guaranteeing no alibis, these possibilities expose the hollowness of the notion that the self can be posited in any one, verifiable position: 'the vacuum of his eyes'. Perhaps ultimately unmanageable, the 'mystery tramp' reflects identity as unsettled, evading fixture and formulation. Always on the move, he has a number of family relations in another lyric from *Highway 61 Revisited*, 'Ballad of a Thin Man'.

'Ballad of a Thin Man' consists simply of a voice scornfully addressing a certain 'Mister Jones': 'something is happening here / But you don't know what it is / Do you, Mister Jones?'. Throughout the lyric Mister Jones is envisaged as one who enters upon a scene – a scene that is never precisely delineated – in which he is out of place and of which he has no knowledge. It is upon questions of knowledge that the speaker's censure of Mister Jones turns. In the first place there is hostility to the gathering of mere information. At the very opening of the lyric: 'You walk into the room / With your pencil in your hand.' The note-taking implied by that pencil is deemed by the speaker incapable of coping with the phenomena Mister Jones now faces:

> You try so hard
> But you don't understand
> Just what you'll say
> When you get home

Though this is not to say that the documentary approach will not turn even more reductively empirical when its inadequacies are pointed out, as the speaker is very well aware:

> You have many contacts
> Among the lumberjacks
> To get you facts
> When someone attacks your imagination

The mind that is sustained by data alone may also be one that proceeds only by cold abstraction. 'You've been with the professors', the speaker tells the unfortunate yet resilient Mister Jones in stanza five:

Mouths

> And they've all liked your looks
> With great lawyers you have
> Discussed lepers and crooks
> You've been through all of
> F. Scott Fitzgerald's books
> You're very well read
> It's well known

Not that F. Scott Fitzgerald is not a proper object of knowledge. The objection in this lyric is to a way of knowing that defines knowledge purely in terms of that which is available to the discursive intellect: 'With great lawyers you have / Discussed lepers and crooks.' With insiders, in other words, you have debated outsiders. But the satiric insinuation is of the absence in such discussions of an imaginative comprehension of conditions of alienation.

From one point of view 'Ballad of a Thin Man' constitutes an attack on an ideology of rationalism, in much the same vein as the speaker of 'Tombstone Blues', also from *Highway 61 Revisited*, declares:

> Now I wish I could write you a melody so plain
> That could hold you dear lady from going insane
> That could ease you and cool you and cease the pain
> Of your useless and pointless knowledge

In 'Tombstone Blues' the sensuality of the young – relatively free of inscribed knowledge – may temporarily unsettle authorized orders and abstractions: 'The geometry of innocence flesh on the bone / Causes Galileo's math book to get thrown'. But the 'king of the Philistines . . . / Puts the pied pipers in prison' and in this lyric it remains an open question whether freedom from a cultural dead hand will not always be betrayed into servitude:

Mouths

> The geometry of innocence flesh on the bone
> Causes Galileo's math book to get thrown
> At Delilah who sits worthlessly alone
> But the tears on her cheeks are from laughter

In 'Ballad of a Thin Man' an ideology of rationalism is apprehended, in the first place, in external terms. It dramatizes, with an acid wit, a scene where the representative of a dominant, rationalistic culture encounters another kind of culture (or, perhaps, subculture). But such encounters, recognizable in their outward features, do not happen only at the surface of things. Nor are the players in the drama necessarily just different kinds of people. The tension between opposing forces in 'Ballad of a Thin Man' may be played out within the individual mind and, at the same time as the lyric visualizes an external confrontation, it enacts that confrontation as an interior drama, as a matter of the rational self's repression of deeper impulses of personality. The limitations of such a repression are not merely asserted in the lyric. They are demonstrated at those points where Mister Jones is brought up against things that cannot simply be rationalized. Most striking are his encounters with a series of figures drawn from the tradition of circus or carnival. In the third stanza, 'You hand in your ticket / And you go watch the geek';[3] in the sixth, 'the sword swallower, he comes up to you'; and in the seventh, 'Now you see this one-eyed midget.' These figures invoke the freely creative, if anarchic, potencies of the imagination. Confronting them, Mister Jones is put in the position of negotiating 'something' that is 'happening' deeper than the reach of merely the rational self. No doubt the antitypes of his conversations with professors and lawyers, his encounters with them comprise darkly funny exercises in confronting the absurd:

Mouths

> you go watch the geek
> Who immediately walks up to you
> When he hears you speak
> And says, 'How does it feel
> To be such a freak?'
> And you say, 'Impossible'
> As he hands you a bone
>
> the sword swallower, he comes up to you
> And then he kneels
> He crosses himself
> And then he clicks his high heels
> And without further notice
> He asks you how it feels
> And he says, 'Here is your throat back
> Thanks for the loan'

Language marks the divide that is dramatized in 'Ballad of a Thin Man' between the conscious self and unconscious potentiality. A series of present-tense verbs thinly disguises the fact that these episodes involving Mister Jones and the carnival figures are deficient in normal causal connections. As the 'geek', 'sword swallower', and 'one-eyed midget' present a challenge to reason and the rational self so they challenge the logical sequences of syntax. There is in each episode a disturbance of predictable lexical arrangement. And, as words are displaced from their usual contexts, the straightfoward meaning, the assumed transparency, of the most ordinary words and speech patterns is called into question. It is an independence which would render them opaque to the eye attempting to read them according to customary usage. Dylan's passages achieve a surrealist effect in which the rebellion of words becomes a measure of the rebellion of the imagination against rational censorship. A notable moment of collision with syntactic control comes in the seventh stanza as the 'one-eyed midget', abrogating the accepted continuities of dialogue, seeks to cut the connection so desperately insisted upon by Mister Jones between reason, meaning and language:

> Now you see this one-eyed midget
> Shouting the word 'NOW'
> And you say, 'For what reason?'
> And he says, 'How?'
> And you say, 'What does this mean?'
> And he screams back, 'You're a cow
> Give me some milk
> Or else go home'

At once vital and grave ('you say, "Impossible" / As he hands you a bone'), Dylan's comic-grotesque figures are instinct with that carnival laughter which, in the words of Mikhail Bakhtin, is 'gay, triumphant, and at the same time mocking and deriding', which 'asserts and denies. . . . buries and revives'.[4] They are informed by the carnival spirit that, in its hostility to all that is 'completed', exposes the 'gay relativity of prevailing truths and authorities'.[5] But only to some degree. Dylan's exotic carnival figures are shown finally to be in no position to celebrate an unconditional emancipation from established orders. And the domestic Mister Jones, while disconcerted at glimpsing what it is to be without a home, remains unrepentant. It is with complacent indignation that he reacts to the momentary disruption in stanza two of a usual pattern of interrogative exchange:

> You raise up your head
> And you ask, 'Is this where it is?'
> And somebody points to you and says
> 'It's his'
> And you say, 'What's mine?'

> And somebody else says, 'Where what is?'
> And you say, 'Oh my God
> Am I here all alone?'

Mister Jones is here led to put inadvertently what could be construed as a radical question about identity, about what may be said to belong to the self. But Mister Jones would be blind to such a construction. The attempted disorientation of his terms of reference throughout the lyric never succeeds in reconstituting him within a discourse by which he might reread the entire question, 'What's mine?' Endorsing reason and meaning even to the end Mister Jones remains closed to the imaginative possibilities erupting before him. Equally, however, this very resilience denies unqualified potentiality to the forces that refuse to conform to the rules of his rationality.

What is crucial in the lyric is that the relationship between those forces and those rules is not a matter of mutual indifference. Each side behaves as if under compulsion to confront the other. And it is more than a matter of simple opposition. While the figures of carnival and Mister Jones appear caught in stark contrast at the surface level of the lyric the narrative itself contains elements which collapse any absolute distinction between them. Mister Jones never gives up hope of being able to frame order out of chaos. The 'one-eyed midget' assumes the possibility of exploiting – even drawing some kind of sustenance from – Mister Jones: '"Give me some milk."' Mister Jones may also have something that the 'sword swallower' needs, however disparagingly the sword swallower may phrase his gratitude for the satisfaction of that need: '"Here is your throat back / Thanks for the loan."' Conversely, the sword swallower's asking Mister Jones how 'it feels' and his thanking Mister Jones for the use of his 'throat' add up to a picture of Mister Jones as a swallower of swords. Mister Jones and the sword swallower may be at odds with each other but only in the special sense that different dimensions of one psyche may be at odds with each other. There is a comparable effect when the 'geek', inverting the obvious terms, asks Mister Jones how it feels to be a 'freak'. But the different personae of the lyric discover their interconnections most tellingly in the speaker's own final perception of Mister Jones. In the closing stanza of the lyric Mister Jones is no longer envisioned simply as the narrow man defined by a world of 'facts' and 'books' and a society of 'professors' and 'lawyers'. Instead he appears to the speaker in the guise of the absurd itself:

> Well, you walk into the room
> Like a camel and then you frown
> You put your eyes in your pocket
> And your nose on the ground

While 'Ballad of a Thin Man' speaks, from one point of view, as a one-sided assault, its deepest sensitivity is to the interdependence of the rational and the irrational, the interinvolvement of meaning and the absurd. That the lyric speaks at all presumes the necessity of that interdependence. Julia Kristeva has said that literature of the avant-garde, a modernist literature characterized by teasing perversions of logical construction, is a kind of writing in which the energies of the unconscious graphically break through the strict, constraining orders of reason: 'Magic, shamanism, esoterism, the carnival, and "incomprehensible" poetry all underscore the limits of socially useful discourse and attest to what it represses.'[6] But repressor and repressed cannot simply be divorced. The energies of imagination that are felt within a literary text may be 'indifferent to language, enigmatic'.[7] They may constitute a 'space underlying the written' that is 'rhythmic, unfettered ... musical, anterior to judgement', but it is a space that is 'restrained by a single

Mouths

guarantee: syntax'.[8] It is a space necessarily restrained, if not contained, because such restraint is the condition of intelligibility. Speaking of the interrelations between the irrational and the rational in poetry Kristeva invokes Mallarmé's view of the '"mysterious" functioning of literature as a rhythm made intelligible by syntax'.[9] In 'Ballad of a Thin Man', however much they may rail against an arid rationalism, and however much they espouse the cause of a surrealist subversion, the lyric and its speaker never entirely divest themselves of the rational syntax of language. 'Ballad of a Thin Man' refuses, ultimately, to allow that imagination or the unconscious are able to speak in a way that is not complicit in the language that defines Mister Jones. In the last resort no hard separation is allowed between reason and imagination. Speaker and lyric, for they are one and the same, are implied simultaneously in the beings of Mister Jones and the carnival figures.

Yet the dialectic in 'Ballad of a Thin Man' is never finally resolvable. The work comes to a conclusion by an arbitrary act of establishing an ending. But as a drama of the relation between reason and free creative desire, between language and the unconscious, the lyric's text is endless. Syntax will continue to attempt to rein in the asyntactic, which will in turn continue to slip complete harnessing. The sword swallower's gratitude for the loan of Mister Jones's throat, the instrument and mechanism of utterance, also conceals a recognition that imagination's articulation is coincident with Mister Jones's language. The mutual suspicion involved in this transaction images a negotiation between interests that are inextricably linked but not conformable to each other. The relationship between Mister Jones and the forces of carnival is one of tense interaction that never achieves a synthesis. It is a relationship that, as a paradigm of the connections between language and the unconscious, becomes a paradigm of the lyric itself. The next chapter will show how the

Mouths

further implications of such a paradigm are explored in lyrics by Dylan – including 'Eternal Circle' (1963), 'Mr. Tambourine Man' and 'Love Minus Zero/No Limit' (*BABH*) – which take as their immediate subject the creative processes by which they are themselves brought into being.

3
Reels of Rhyme

> I walk across the bridge in the dismal light
> Where all the cars are stripped between the gates of night.
> I see the trembling lion with the lotus flower tail
> And then I kiss your lips as I lift your veil.
> But you're gone and then all I seem to recall is the
>   smell of perfume
> And your golden loom.
>
> 'Golden Loom' (1975)

'I don't know', said Dylan of the composition of 'Mr. Tambourine Man', 'different things inspired me. . . .'[1] Different things, no doubt, and in another sense nothing external to inspiration itself. When the speaker of 'Mr. Tambourine Man' invites the Tambourine Man to 'play a song for me', he is inviting himself to a mystery. 'Take me', the speaker says, 'on a trip upon your magic swirlin' ship.' To hear the song would be to embark on an interior voyage. What the speaker desires is the chance 'to fade/Into my own parade': 'take me disappearin' through the smoke rings of my mind.' Within the fiction of the lyric the address to the Tambourine Man is an address made by the self to the self. Specifically, Tambourine Man is called upon as a figure of the imaginative self or creative soul of the poet-speaker. The energy with which he is associated is the inspirational energy of artistic creation. In the third stanza the achievement of poetic form is envisaged as resting upon the measure of the Tambourine Man's music: 'skippin' reels of rhyme / To your tambourine in time'. 'Mr. Tambourine Man', as one commentator has aptly summarized, is a poet's 'invocation to his muse'.[2]

Muses, however, are not made to order. The point is highlighted in 'Mr. Tambourine Man' by the way in which the governing verb of the refrain, '*play* a song for me', repeated ten times in the course of the lyric, becomes as much a plea as an injunction. The effect is reinforced by the repetition of the demand to be taken – 'Take me on a trip', 'take me disappearin'' – where the command is a request to be taken command of. In the last line of the last stanza the imperative is a demand for permission: 'Let me forget . . .'. Inspiration, it is implied, is is something to be managed and simultaneously submitted to; something that can be directed but which is at the same time so coyly indirect in its agency that it must be cajoled into ravishing.

At one level, 'Mr. Tambourine Man' comprises an account of what it is to be inspired from the immediate vantage point of not being so. Such distance is appropriate to a power that is figured throughout the lyric – if not as the divine thing of classical metaphor for the source and nature of inspiration – then at least as preternatural in character. The images of the final stanza especially convey a sense of something which moves and has its being deeper than the quotidian world and self and which escapes strictly logical formulation. To be drawn by the tambourine music is to draw deeply on the unconscious, whose edges cannot be fixed. It is to negotiate the limits of finite structures, to the point where these begin to break down ('the . . . ruins of time') and where objects of common experience are, as it were, petrified by a more-than-natural energy ('frozen leaves, / . . . frightened trees'). To be assumed into the force of the creative moment would be to suspend ordinary suffering:

> Then take me disappearin' through the smoke rings of
>   my mind,
> Down the foggy ruins of time, far past the frozen leaves,
> The haunted, frightened trees, out to the windy beach,
> Far from the twisted reach of crazy sorrow.

The apotheosis envisaged in the remaining lines of this stanza has several defining features. There is the 'diamond sky': the crystalline perfection of an aestheticized nature. Like the 'Marbles of the dancing floor' in the City of Yeats's 'Byzantium', Dylan's 'diamond sky' is intimidating in its cold, unyielding brilliance. But its worth lies precisely in its transmutation of natural laws. The dance that takes place beneath this sky is an ecstatic one, the possessed dance of the creative moment itself, something larger than self-consciousness and reason. Imagination at this point overrides 'memory and fate', affirms a scope beyond the time-bound determinism of the natural self. And again an image of circus finds its place in a picture of the subversion of the established and the known:

> Yes, to dance beneath the diamond sky with one
>   hand waving free,
> Silhouetted by the sea, circled by the circus sands,
> With all memory and fate driven deep beneath the waves,
> Let me forget about today until tomorrow.

The expression of the last line – its anxiety *about* time spoken from the perspective of the self *in* time – reminds us that the force of the dance is indeed only envisaged. However much the words of this lyric may predict the 'ruins of time' the lyric itself is committed in its rhyme-scheme to the pleasures of anticipation and recollection and remains structured in time. The wish to suppress memory and fate touches a wish that rhyme itself – a mnemonic device grounded in the predeterminations of repetition – be suppressed. But a yearning to be 'free' is contradicted by the temporal gratifications offered in the rhyme with 'sea'. In this instance, as throughout, the lyric simultaneously contemplates and refuses its own ruination. The desired transcendence conflicts with the contingency of the language and form by which such transcendence is posited. It is a tension ironically caught in the rhyme that orders the image of the relationship between poetic measure and a preternatural energy: 'skippin' reels of rhyme / To your tambourine in time.'

A contrast between statements concerning freedom and the boundaries of rhyme is something frequently exploited by Dylan. In 'Abandoned Love' (1975; *Biograph*), for example, rhyme merely confirms the speaker's conviction of an actual, if not publicly acknowledged, entrapment: 'I march in the parade of liberty / But as long as I love you I'm not free.' Again, 'Subterranean Homesick Blues' (*BABH*) voices a characteristic American dread that in the land of the free individual freedom has been misplaced. In this lyric the nervously abbreviated lines and the overinsistencies of alliteration and rhyme register the sense of a culture's stunting of the possibilities of individual growth. In the second stanza, even the life of the underground remains oppressively patterned, imprisoned in its paranoia about authority:

> Maggie comes fleet foot
> Face full of black soot
> Talkin' that the heat put
> Plants in the bed but
> The phone's tapped anyway

> Maggie says that many say
> They must bust in early May
> Orders from the D.A.
> Look out kid
> Don't matter what you did
> Walk on your tip toes
>
> . . . . .
>
> You don't need a weather man
> To know which way the wind blows

A love lyric such as 'You're Gonna Make Me Lonesome When You Go' (*BT*) shows its speaker acutely conscious of past, present and future:

> Situations have ended sad,
> Relationships have all been bad.
> Mine've been like Verlaine's and Rimbaud.
> But there's no way I can compare
> All those scenes to this affair,
> Yer gonna make me lonesome when you go.

And when in this song a claim is made, true to the rhetoric of love, that it is possible to rise above a sense of time passing it is a claim playfully undercut by a rhyme on time: 'Crickets talkin' back and forth in rhyme, / . . . / I could stay with you forever / And never realise the time.' The boundaries of the time-defined, conscious self are not easily transgressed. In 'Mr. Tambourine Man' the sense of strain in the image of a repression of memory and fate ('driven deep beneath the waves') hints at a sense in which the conscious will may co-operate only anxiously in a yearning for its own suspension.

But yearning can itself be part of a process of preparation and 'Mr. Tambourine Man' says a great deal about the nature of the preparation that is needed if the imaginative moment is to come. Just as, in Yeats's 'Byzantium', the 'mummy-cloth' of mortal experience must be unwound from the 'bobbin' of the soul before Byzantium can be reached, so Dylan's lyric envisages a purgation of the ordinary self as the necessary prelude to hearing the music of the tambourine. The second stanza describes the conditionless state that is yet the condition of being able to hear the music and to dance the dance:

> My senses have been stripped, my hands can't feel to grip,
> My toes too numb to step . . .
> I'm ready to go anywhere, I'm ready for to fade
> Into my own parade, cast your dancing spell my way . . .

It is a state, as the first stanza suggests, distinguishable from the dominion of worldly things – a dominion whose transience is measured in the hour-glass: 'I know that evenin's empire has returned into sand, / Vanished from my hand' – a state of spiritual endazzlement transcending literal sight and natural inclination to rest; the condition of a solitary vision more intense than the dreams of the mortal sleeper:

> Left . . . blindly here to stand but still not sleeping.
> My weariness amazes me, I'm branded on my feet,
> I have no one to meet
> And the ancient empty street's too dead for dreaming.

All this aching, however, only directs us to the paradox upon which 'Mr. Tambourine Man' is built. As a lyric the work itself evidences an attainment of the creative moment which its speaker spends so much time anticipating. In this sense, the lyric-speaker's pursuit of an energy located in the future turns out to be a pursuit of the lyric's own origin. That which is desired has, in

Reels of Rhyme

the writing of the desire in poetic language, already been achieved. The desire is fulfilled in the writing of the lyric. For the speaker to stop speaking would be to fail in the realization of his desire. But this also means, paradoxically, that there is a sense in which it becomes impossible to conceive of a complete fulfilment, a fulfilment to end all fulfilments. The dance is in the writing and the writing is in the dance and this is why there is never a final word, never a place (except in death) where it would be possible to leave off writing. Writing could be phrased as a looking for a final or ultimate word. But that would be pure word, the Word before words. Such a Word shadows writing, it is writing's inspiration. But while it both energizes and is pursued by writing the Word is never simply contained by words. It is, as it were, a ghost in the machine, at once seductively beckoning and mockingly elusive.

A haunting image in the third stanza of 'Mr. Tambourine Man' is committed to exploring the sense in which the mystery of inspiration is the mystery of language. The speaker is attempting on this occasion to reassure the Tambourine Man:

And if you hear vague traces of skippin' reels of rhyme
To your tambourine in time, it's just a ragged clown behind,
I wouldn't pay it any mind, it's just a shadow you're
Seein' that he's chasing.

If Tambourine Man is a figure of the energy of inspiration, the lyric-speaker here finds, in the persona of the 'ragged clown', a figure for the self that has been inspired, the self that produces aesthetic form. It is a self constituted in its very productions, as is suggested in the way the construction and punctuation of the verse insist upon an identification of 'reels of rhyme' with 'clown'. Both rhyme and clown undergo a similar identification with the 'shadow' in the third line of the passage. Yet the clown is almost simultaneously pictured at a remove from – as, indeed, 'chasing' – the shadow. The shadow might be read as that of Tambourine Man, but it might just as well be read as the clown's own shadow. Tambourine Man and clown, sharing one shadow, are as distinguishable and inseparable as inspiration and the inspired self might be expected to be. And just as Tambourine Man is implied in the shadow and the clown, so he is implied in the 'rhyme', the inspired language, that is interchangeable with the clown and the shadow. The drama of this gnomically self-reflexive image enacts the way in which the Word and the word, inspirational energy and the poetic self and its creations, imply each other without ever being literally one and the same thing. Poetic language and poetic power chase each other in a circle of mutual implication, an incessant shadow-play. Poetic language, and the self that makes and is made by that language, trace an energy that is represented by the Tambourine Man and his music. But it is a tracing that, like all tracing, neither completely defines nor is utterly divorced from what it traces. Tambourine Man himself is inscribed in the language of 'Mr. Tambourine Man', but as the essential Word is not held once and for all time by these particular words. Dylan's image conveys a sense of poetry as generated in a compulsive and never to be literally fulfilled cycle of desire for a meeting between language and essence, conscious and unconscious, word and Word. The logical absurdity of the compulsion directs the casting of the poetic self in the figure of the clown.

Yet for all his raggedness the clown is by no means to be pitied. The speaker's attempt to reassure Tambourine Man can invert priority of value in respect of Tambourine Man and the 'skippin' reels of rhyme'. The felt need to reassure has the odd and lovely effect of celebrating the dignity of the tracing, the 'reels of rhyme' themselves, the achieved art-form. Such celebration is an integral part of the lyric's self-celebration – a self-celebration that is one

Reels of Rhyme

of the prime functions of the third stanza. The opening lines of this stanza characterize the state of daemonic possession as a joyful emancipation from constraint, including even the constraint of responsibility to an audience. As the speaker addresses Tambourine Man a disorientation of accustomed perceptual and sensory points of reference is suggested through an image of motion – spinning and swinging – along two different axes simultaneously:

> Though you might hear laughin', spinnin', swingin'
>   madly across the sun,
> It's not aimed at anyone, it's just escapin' on the run
> And but for the sky there are no fences facin'.

What is distinctive here is that the speaker does not, as in the first two and the last stanzas, simply look forward, insisting on his own preparedness. The possibility of Tambourine Man hearing the music might be read as a future possibility. But there follows a striking use of present and present continuous tenses. Not 'it *would* not *be* aimed' but 'it *is* not aimed.' Similarly, in the passage that concludes the stanza, it *is* a ragged clown *chasing* a shadow. The shift in this stanza out of the temporal logic of the rest of the lyric on one hand enhances the universalization of the reflection on poetry contained in the image of rhyme, clown, shadow and Tambourine Man. On the other hand, the placing of the image in a kind of perpetual present enables it to reflect directly on the lyric in which it occurs. The laughing, the spinning, the swinging and the chasing are what is happening as this lyric is being written.

The return to a future oriented perspective in the last stanza allows the work once again to look outward beyond itself to other creative trips, to lyrics yet to be written. The sense of an endlessly repeatable pattern of beginning anew with Tambourine Man, of endless possibilities of writing and rewriting the Word, is conveyed in the open-endedness of a refrain that is reiterated without variation five times in the course of the lyric. It is an effect of open-endedness that is emphasized by the performative elements of the song. In the rendering of 'Mr. Tambourine Man' on *Bringing It All Back Home* the lightly sounding cadences at the end of each section continually forestall musical closure:

> Hey! Mr. Tambourine Man, play a song for me,
> I'm not sleepy and there is no place I'm going to.
> Hey! Mr. Tambourine Man, play a song for me,
> In the jingle jangle morning I'll come followin' you.

In its expression of a desire to be possessed 'Mr. Tambourine Man' passes as a special kind of love lyric. The kind of love in which it deals is often re-explored in Dylan's work and the casting of Tambourine Man as an inspirational figure is complemented by the use of female figures to fulfil a comparable role. Writing in *New Society* in 1970, Christopher Ballantine noticed Tambourine Man's spiritual peers when he spoke of a class of love lyrics 'addressed to no earthly woman' but to 'Dylan's muse'.[3] One of the earliest of such lyrics, the 1963 'Eternal Circle', anticipates elements of 'Mr. Tambourine Man' in its recognition of a principle of recurrent creative beginnings.

At a literal level 'Eternal Circle' speaks of a singer who, whilst performing, watches and is watched by a woman who disappears once the performance is over. Beneath its surface *naïveté* the lyric establishes subtle correlations between the activity of artistic expression and a symbolic female figure. In the first stanza the presence of this figure, dimly apprehended at the tentative outset of the singing, is fully realized only as the piece gets properly underway, only as the production of the song turns metaphorically into a spinning – a creative dance and an aesthetic weave.

> I sang the song slowly
> As she stood in the shadows
> She stepped to the light
> As my silver strings spun
> She called with her eyes
> To the tune I's a-playin'

In the last two lines of this passage the figure's relationship is pointedly with the art and not in any simple sense with the singer, just as in the following stanza:

> Her face was reflectin'
> The fast fading words
> That rolled from my tongue

In the fourth verse the female figure's 'thoughts' are referred to in a way that places them as much inside as outside the singer-speaker's consciousness. Here, as throughout the lyric, 'she' serves figuratively as a projection of the creative spirit at work in the singing of the song. At this level the fourth verse speaks of the artist's need to attend to the dictates – dictates of the mind at once felt along the heart – of his own imaginative impulse:

> I glanced at my guitar
> And played it pretendin'
> That of all the eyes out there
> I could see none
> As her thoughts pounded hard
> Like the pierce of an arrow

Yet if she is the embodiment of the singer-speaker's own creative self, she is also a figure of the inspired work of art itself.

Reels of Rhyme

Her thoughts pulse hard as the force informing artistic expression. But her face also mirrors – constitutes an image of – the achieved words of the song. It is in this sense that we perceive the aesthetic implications of the opening lines of the third stanza, 'My eyes danced a circle / Across her clear outline', where the perception of her outline might be read as defining the singer's apprehension of the formal achievement of the song he is singing. But this lyric has not yet been danced out and the sense of the woman not merely calling to but calling the tune, calling it into being, is picked up in the succeeding lines. Not that her role in such calling can be quantified. As an inspirational figure she is enigmatically beckoning, teasingly enticing. Neither exactly one with singer or with song she inhabits and breathes through both at an elusive, pentecostal remove:

> With her head tilted sideways
> She called me again
> As the tune drifted out
> She breathed hard through the echo

Each stanza of 'Eternal Circle' comes to an end with a 'But'. In the second, her eyes were 'on fire / But the song it was long / And there was more to be sung.' The third has 'But . . . it was far to the end' and the fourth 'But . . . it had to get done.' Taken literally the point might be that singer and woman cannot approach each other until the performance is finished. Yet something else is captured in the repetition of the conjunction and in the phrases it introduces. The 'But's might seem to indicate the frustration of one kind of mutual desire. But there is no such obvious frustration when in the first stanza, for instance, she 'called with her eyes / To the tune I's a-playin' / But the song it was long / And I'd only begun.' The calling is to the tune and the singer knows it, so that the length of the song, rather than a cause for frustration, could have been thought a cause for satisfaction. Similarly, in the third stanza her breath mingles with the breath of the voice that utters the words of the song, while in the fourth her thoughts are assimilated to the singer-speaker. The two effectively meet, coalesce, within the medium of the song itself. Yet even with such identification taking place in the context of the creative act the demurring 'But's still keep coming. At the figurative level of the lyric the conjunctions help to define a sense in which the female figure, as the projection of the inspiring agency, is touched through the creative realization of the artistic work but at the same time is not finally possessed in and by this work. The closing of the circle of this song, its completion, does not close the larger cycle – the eternal, temporally unclosable circle of creativity – within which the work has its beginning and its end. As an object of desire, beckoning towards creation, the creative spirit is realized in this song and simultaneously, lest that spirit be utterly exorcised with the creation of this work, she always lies beyond it, like echo to a sound or shadow to the figure which casts it. In the story of 'Eternal Circle' this spirit evaporates when the song is over. Neither permanently defining nor forever defined by a single work, she must always bring into being and be brought into being by another creative act. Thus, in the fifth and last stanza, there is a different placing for and a different kind of 'But':

> As the tune finally folded
> I laid down the guitar
> Then looked for the girl
> Who'd stayed for so long
> But her shadow was missin'
> For all of my searchin'
> So I picked up my guitar
> And began the next song.

'Eternal Circle' addresses itself to the manner in which artistic fulfilment is always at once a disappointment. The position of the greatest gain, when formlessness or silence are redeemed in the completion of a work of art, is simultaneously a position of loss. It may seem, on one hand, a long way to the end of the song but, on the other, there is anxious recognition of the principle of perpetual loss and constant deferral of fulfilment as the singer-speaker comments in the second verse of the lyric on his 'fast fading words'. The process is one whereby that which is realized in the generation of form fades as rapidly as the form is produced. Picturing the mysterious 'she' that is another self as never utterly possessed in the singing yet as disappearing utterly when the singing ends, 'Eternal Circle' pictures the dynamic of poetic creation: the necessity of always pursuing through 'matter moulded forms of speech'[4] that which forever eludes those forms; the necessity of always searching for a temporally untraceable origin and a temporally unrealizable end. It is the paradoxical dynamic of poetic creation that is registered when, in another of Dylan's lyrics to present the imaginative daemon in feminine form, the 'she' of 'Love Minus Zero/No Limit' is said to know 'there's no success like failure / And that failure's no success at all'.

The creative self which impassions the speaker of 'Love Minus Zero/No Limit' is characterized throughout the lyric in terms of paradox. The terms locate a potency that in itself is neither susceptible to logical analysis nor measurable according to social norms. In the first line the creative self is said to use a language that is at least enigmatic: 'My love she speaks like silence.' The very title to the lyric attributes a mode of transcendence to the love in question: 'Love Minus Zero' – a love from which nothing may be taken. But since nought is in any case not a figure that can be subtracted from anything it is a love that eludes empirical, quantitative assessment. It has, like the mystic eternality of the zero in 'Eternal Circle', no limit. Having neither the aspirations nor the unregeneracy of the ordinary world it is of an extreme veracity that has nothing to do with obliged and hence circumscribed faith:

> My love she speaks like silence,
> Without ideals or violence,
> She doesn't have to say she's faithful,
> Yet she's true, like ice, like fire.

The next four lines of this opening stanza, recalling the possessed laughter of the fruitful moment in 'Mr. Tambourine Man', also include an association that recurs throughout Dylan's work between the creative soul (or poetry itself) and 'flowers'. Flowers as a general category, rather than the individual flower – the rose, for instance – with its socially specific symbolism. The speaker contrasts his love both with the fickleness of conventional protestations of lasting devotion and with all conceptions of love as a contractable commodity:

> People carry roses,
> Make promises by the hours,
> My love she laughs like the flowers,
> Valentines can't buy her.

Both the second and third stanzas contrast the speaker's love with worldly debates, preoccupations and principles. The second uses paradox to highlight the futility of expecting consummation – of attempting to fix final ends – in time:

> In the dime stores and bus stations,
> People talk of situations,
> Read books, repeat quotations,
> Draw conclusions on the wall.

> Some speak of the future,
> My love she speaks softly,
> She knows there's no success like failure
> And that failure's no success at all.

In the third stanza the creative self is pictured as slyly indifferent to the burlesque shows of potency and the frail edifices of power belonging to the public world:

> The cloak and dagger dangles,
> Madams light the candles.
> In ceremonies of the horsemen,
> Even the pawn must hold a grudge.
> Statues made of match sticks,
> Crumble into one another,
> My love winks, she does not bother,
> She knows too much to argue or to judge.

Such a love, however, is not necessarily borne lightly. Subverting logic and convention the daemon is not reducible to a tame or sentimental sweetness. Even in his most enthusiastic celebrations of the poetic muse, Dylan's graces can bear a troubling aspect. There may not be a mundane violence in the 'love' of 'Love Minus Zero/No Limit' but, in a redeployment of Petrarchan conceit, she freezes and burns 'like ice, like fire'. Similarly, in his preparation for the ecstatic dance the speaker of 'Mr. Tambourine Man' is blinded, numbed, stripped, 'branded' on his feet. Suffering is recognized as part of the creative process in the image of the wounding spirit in 'Eternal Circle', whose 'thoughts pounded hard / Like the pierce of an arrow'. The last stanza of 'Love Minus Zero/No Limit', opening with the disconcerting shudder of 'The bridge at midnight trembles', ushers in a potently ambivalent image of the creative principle. The third and fourth lines of this stanza mock an expectation of grace as something that is proprietorially due and which may be safely appropriated: 'Bankers' nieces seek perfection, / Expecting all the gifts that wise men bring.' In the succeeding four lines creative inspiration is figured as a forge that would shatter all such shallow conceptions of perfection. The daemon herself comes as an ominous harbinger, witness to a dangerous, potentially unmanageable force. And yet, lest the nature of that preternatural force be crudely misconceived, the creative spirit is figured as coming at once as an emissary of delicate vulnerability, something that may itself be damaged, something that may energize beyond all forms of social containment and at the same time stand in need of nurturing:

> The wind howls like a hammer,
> The night blows cold and rainy,
> My love she's like some raven
> At my window with a broken wing.

The nervous exultation and the tension between inspiration and form intrinsic to Dylan's vision of the processes of artistic creation find analogies, as the next chapter will attempt to show, in those of his lyrics which open out into an exploration of the workings of the psyche as a whole.

4

Lady Language Creator

> Escape me?
> Never –
> Beloved!
> While I am I, and you are you, –
> So long as the world contains us both,
> Me the loving and you the loth,
> While the one eludes, must the other pursue...
> I shape me –
> Ever
> Removed!
>
> Robert Browning, 'Life in a Love'

'To Isis Moon Lady Language Creator Birth Goddess, Mother of Ra, Saraswati & Aphrodite, Divine Mother.' Thus Allen Ginsberg in a note accompanying the lyric 'Isis' on the 1976 record that Dylan entitled, simply, *Desire*.[1] Ginsberg's gloss identifies some of the principal mythological and symbolic motifs – motifs rich in psychological implication – that are invoked in 'Isis'. They are motifs invoked and reworked in a lyric that exploits the form of the lyrical ballad to provide a dramatic monologue of the desires and drives that go to constitute individual identity. They are desires and drives that are seen, ultimately, as overwhelming the pale of reason. In the final stanza:

Isis, oh, Isis, you mystical child.
What drives me to you is what drives me insane.

The story of 'Isis' turns on division. The first line of the lyric has its speaker recounting a union: 'I married Isis on the fifth day of May.' The second line records a separation: 'But I could not hold on to her very long.' The lyric's narrative then relates a fantastic journey – into 'wild unknown country' as far as a tomb containing an empty casket – undertaken by the speaker following the failure of his relationship with Isis. The furthest stage of the journey having been retold, the narrative circles back on itself until in the penultimate stanza it recalls Isis and the speaker meeting again.

'I married Isis on the fifth day of May.' May – the month of spring fertility rites, the time when Hermes led Persephone out of Hades back to her mother Demeter. The connotations of May are fused in the first line of 'Isis' with the numerological significances involved in the specification of the fifth day of the fifth month of the Gregorian calendar. One of the numbers associated with the universal figure of the Great Goddess, the type of generative power, five is the number of Demeter, of Ishtar, Aphrodite, and of Isis herself. The number five contributes moreover to the interweaving of May with the topic of marriage. For five is also the mystic number of the *hieros gamos*, the archetypal Sacred Marriage of Heaven and Earth, the fruitful union of opposites, of sun and moon, of male and female principles.[2] In its psychological resonance such a marriage may represent the harmonious union of different elements – both conscious and unconscious – of the personality. 'To Isis Moon Lady . . . Divine Mother.' In 'Isis' the persona of the goddess appears under one aspect as a type of the 'feminine' dimension of identity. Goddess of fertility, a divinity of the moon, she is a figure of elemental resource and unconscious potentiality. In this respect she weds the speaker as

Lady Language Creator

soul mate, as anima to his 'masculine' self. In the marriage on the fifth day of May resides an *image* of a state of completed desire, of wholeness, of unified personality. A survey of the main features of the narrative will enable a more detailed tracing of the motif of psychological division and reunification in 'Isis', though such a motif, as this discussion will go on to suggest, far from controls the range of signification in the lyric.

The speaker's splitting away from Isis is marked by a ritualistic act of head-shaving – echoing ancient cult practice – that implies at once a loss of creative energy and a purification, a stage in the preparation for the renewal of that energy:

> I could not hold on to her very long.
> So I cut off my hair and I rode straight away
> For the wild unknown country where I could not go wrong.

The ride that continues both the penance and the preparation is also one that exemplifies the 'masculine' virtues. The speaker in his journey to the tomb and the casket conforms in crucial respects to the archetype of the hero engaged in the labours and aspirations of the quest. The orientation is established in the second stanza. Here, a setting structured around simple binary oppositions hints at the stereotypical narratives of male prowess belonging to the Western:

> I came to a high place of darkness and light.
> The dividing line ran through the center of town.
> I hitched up my pony to a post on the right . . .

Traditionally the masculine side, the right hand is also affiliated with the masculine principle represented by the sun, symbol of conscious strength, of will and rational enlightenment. It is an affiliation rehearsed in 'Isis' as a bearing 'right' is aligned through rhyme with a sympathy for the 'light'.

It is in the context of such bearing and sympathy that the speaker encounters a mysterious stranger who promises a quest-objective and who then accompanies the speaker in the pursuit of that objective. 'A man', we are told in the third stanza,

> approached me for a match.
> I knew right away he was not ordinary.
> He said, 'Are you lookin' for somethin' easy to catch?'
> I said, 'I got no money'. He said, 'That ain't necessary'.

Nor, it seems, given the light of fellow feeling struck between the two men, was more detailed explanation necessary. In stanza four:

We set out that night for the cold in the North.
I gave him my blanket, he gave me his word.
I said, 'Where are we goin'?' He said we'd be back by the fourth.
I said, 'That's the best news that I've ever heard'.

As speaker and stranger ride together, crassly materialistic projections concerning the riches to be gained at the end of the fabulous journey shape themselves oddly into a figuring of a type of resurrection from the dead. In the fifth and seventh stanzas:

I was thinkin' about diamonds and the world's biggest necklace.
As we rode through the canyons, through the devilish cold . . .

We came to the pyramids all embedded in ice.
He said, 'There's a body I'm trying to find.
If I carry it out it'll bring a good price'.

But the intended grave-robbing turns into a funeral. The story tells how the stranger, somewhat precipitately, died. Discovering the tomb to be devoid of all wealth the speaker, far from helping to carry a body out, carries one in. From this pivotal point of the narrative commences the return phase of the speaker's journey. Stanzas eight to ten have the details:

> The wind it was howlin' and the snow was outrageous.
> We chopped through the night and we chopped through the dawn.
> When he died I was hopin' that it wasn't contagious,
> But I made up my mind that I had to go on.
>
> I broke into the tomb but the casket was empty . . .
>
> I picked up his body and I dragged him inside,
> Threw him down in the hole and I put back the cover.
> I said a quick prayer and I felt satisfied.
> Then I rode back to find Isis just to tell her I love her.

'Isis' summarizes the separation/return pattern typical both of quest narratives and of fertility or regeneration myths. The speaker and Isis part after a marriage on the fifth day of May. The mysterious stranger promises the speaker that they will be 'back by the fourth'. The fourth of May? The implied completion of a cycle which would bring the speaker back to his spring starting-point? Certainly the journey away from Isis is marked by a lapse of season. The tomb reached at the point of the journey furthest from the May-day marriage is associated with a landscape of winter: of 'devilish cold', of 'ice' and 'snow'. And just as in vegetation ceremonies there has to be a symbolic death before rebirth is possible, so in 'Isis' the mysterious stranger is consigned to the earth. Death's needs satisfied and a death ritual performed, Isis herself is sought again. Nor is the speaker's remeeting with Isis to be envisaged in merely secular terms. The pattern of nature's eternal return to potency is echoed when in stanza six, as he is well into his journey, the speaker remembers how Isis had told him that 'things would be different the next time we wed'. The *next* time we *wed*. No prophesy here, merely the assumption of a predictable pattern. And not only the next time. After the break-up of the marriage at the opening of the lyric the speaker heads for the 'unknown' country where he 'could not go wrong'. The certainty of going right in unknown conditions hints at his having been there before, at previous separations following previous weddings. In the narrative cycle of the lyric the speaker comes home 'from the East', symbolically the direction of new life, of infancy and spring. It is also the direction of sunrise and the speaker returns *as* the new sun, not so much dazzled as dazzling.

I rode back to find Isis just to tell her I love her.

She was there in the meadow where the creek used to rise . . .
I came in from the East with the sun in my eyes.

In the speaker's return to Isis is imaged again, as in the opening line of the lyric, a sacramental conjunction of sun and moon: a creative union of masculine and female principles.

As a parable of a psychic split, the speaker's journey away from Isis exposes the inadequacies of too one-sided a development of the conventionally masculine aspects of identity. The much-prized attributes of the heroic ego – all will and active self-determination – are stripped to expose an aggressive, imaginatively barren and ultimately life-denying acquisitiveness. In its extreme manifestation it is an ego that must play itself out, that must reach towards its own extinction, before psychic equilibrium and new life can be reapproached. In this way the stranger who is matched with the speaker like a shadow of the self moves towards his own destruction. And like a surrogate sacrifice of the speaker's own negative self it is a death that releases the speaker for his return to Isis.

Lady Language Creator

Considered thus far the drama of 'Isis', with its pattern of mythological reference and symbolic allusion, evokes a familiar model of personal identity. A model which would posit the possibility of resolving different dimensions of personality into a balanced and harmonious whole; which would envision the attainment of a fullness of identity through an integration of the conscious with the unconscious content of the psyche. But while 'Isis' pictures the psyche as a field of conflicting forces or potencies, it does not easily confirm the possibility of a reconciliation of those conflicts. There are energies in the lexical detail and structural arrangement of the lyric which work against the complacencies of resolution or stabilization. They are energies that found expression in the disturbed intensity of Dylan's rendering of 'Isis' at his Rolling Thunder Revue concert in Montreal on 4 December 1975. One of the most powerful of Dylan's recorded live performances it is a rendering that, as Allen Ginsberg notes, the singer had 'developed on stage for weeks whiteface, big grey hat stuck with November leaves & flowers . . .'.[3]

The image of union in 'Isis' constitutes above all an image of the resolution of difference. An image of the union of lover with loved one, of masculine with feminine, of self with soul, it is an image of the suspension of difference between outer and inner, between object and subject. An image of the redemption of self-alienation, it is an image of the assimilation of impurity and incompleteness to ideal form, of complex to archetype. An image of the assimilation of winter to spring, it is, in the last resort, an image of the assimilation of death to life. But what is most important about 'Isis' is that the lyric asserts this image of absolute integration not as a description of a condition finally fulfilled but as an image of desire, an image of a state continually approximated but never achieved. This vision is implicit in the hints within the lyric of repetitive cycles of union, separation and reunion. In their repetition these are relativized conjugations.

They are marriages and remarriages that subvert the notion of a single apocalyptic Wedding. For the lyric to assert the realization of such a transcendent union would be a contradiction in terms. For such a union would preclude the possibilities of discourse itself. So long as the lyric images or speaks of a union it places itself by virtue of its imaging or speaking at a remove from that union; by speaking it does itself divide union. Nor does the speaker of the lyric exist in any simple sense apart from the speaking. The question of identity in 'Isis' is at last inseparable from a question of language.

'To Isis ... Lady Language / Language Creator... Divine Mother.' An image of ideal resource, the pattern of the soul, Isis is only known by virtue of a self-consciousness that is coextensive with language. The 'I' that in this lyric knows itself in relation to another – 'Isis', 'she', 'he', 'you', 'her' – has taken up a position in language. To stand in the self-consciousness and representation of language is to stand always outside the object of reflection and representation. Isis may be the origin of the language by which she is known. But the language by which she is known is also that which divides all who know her from direct, unmediated communion with her. The inability finally to resolve difference, the inability to escape the cycles of separation and return, is above all explored in 'Isis' as an inability to escape language. Known only in language Isis is sought by the 'I' of the lyric as a condition of imaginary unity, a space of pure being which lies anterior to language and to the construction in language of the self-conscious and divided self. She is the pure 'Other' whose possession would complete the self, enable it to possess itself fully, yet only at the self-contradictory cost of dying out of language. Recognized by virtue of and attainable only as a name, or as 'she', 'you' or 'her', full possession of 'Isis' is always deferred by the language that splits the speaking 'I' from participation in undifferentiated being, from absolute self-possession.

The relative status of the 'I' in 'Isis', its inability to fulfil an existence except in relation to others, is emphasized in the lyric's emphasis on the continually shifting quantities of pronoun and person. 'He said, "Are you . . ." . . . I said, "I . . ." He said . . . / We set out . . . I gave him . . . he gave me his . . . I said, "Where are we . . ." . . . He said we'd . . . I said . . . "I've . . ." // . . . she told me . . . we would . . . we wed . . . I only . . . her friend . . . I still . . . she said.' At the moment when speaker and Isis meet again in the penultimate stanza there is a sudden resolution of pronouns into a symmetrical pattern, organized in each line around a pivotal 'I' and offering an approximation of a stabilized and centred self:

> She said, 'Where ya been?' I said, 'No place special'.
> She said, 'You look different'. I said, 'Well, not quite'.
> She said, 'You been gone'. I said, 'That's only natural'.
> She said, 'You gonna stay?' I said, 'Yeah, I jes might'.[4]

But even such resolution does not overcome the difference of she/I and in the discriminations of language the full presence of identity is excluded by *re* presentation. Language and being, I and imago, seeking perfect union, continue to elude each other in these lines. The special irony of the words of Isis remembered by the speaker on his journey, 'things would be different the next time we wed', emerges here. For in the 'reunion' things do not just get better, they just remain different. The principle of difference is emphasized even in the dialogue of this stanza. The moment of the ordering of pronouns, the moment of mutual accord, is shot through with oblique but powerful resistance to perfect communion. The evasive indirection of the speaker's response in the first line disguises an assertion of independence: 'She said, "Where ya been?" I said, "No place special."' Similarly in the second line, the refusal of difference constitutes an endorsement of difference: 'She said, "You look different". I said,

"Well, not quite."' In the third line the confirmation of absence as the principle of a prevailing order empties the subsequent resolution to stay, the commitment to presence, of an absolute ground. It is in any case a qualified commitment that reserves the right to autonomous judgement. '"You been gone". I said, "That's only natural" / . . . "You gonna stay?" I said, "Yeah, I jes might."'

The precariousness of this moment of approximate accord is further apparent in the shift that takes place in the thirteenth and final stanza out of the past tense narrative which has governed the lyric so far. That narrative itself invokes a seasonal cycle and hints not at a final end but at a recurrent pattern of separation and return. But the principle of recurrence is emphasized when in the last stanza of the lyric the voice that has told of union, separation and reunion in the past speaks of a present impulsion towards Isis. The present tense of the 'drives' of the last stanza, which is fixed according to the odd and lunar number thirteen, destroys the finality of the position related in the penultimate stanza and reconstitutes division and the desire for a healing of that division as a continuing condition. The last line of the lyric reminds us of the wedding on the fifth day of May. This is a return to the opening words of the lyric. But it is also a return to Isis's prediction, recalled by the speaker on his journey, concerning their 'next' wedding. With the return to the opening words the story of separation and return may begin again. But marriage as an original, single, absolute event remains an ideal figure haunting words that can never contain what they speak of:

> Isis, oh, Isis, you mystical child.
> What drives me to you is what drives me insane.
> I still can remember the way that you smiled
> On the fifth day of May in the drizzlin' rain.

Language's failure to hold the ideal is one of the preoccupations of 'Isis'. With special emphases and sharpenings the lyric dramatizes the sense in which all language, and the self that exists in language, are necessarily second-hand, alienated, fallen. There are the vulgar vacuities of overstatement: 'I said, "That's the best news that I've ever heard"'; 'I was thinkin' about . . . the world's biggest necklace.' The misprision that is endemic to language is highlighted through specific exploitations of language in 'Isis'. 'When he died I was hopin' that it wasn't contagious.' Whatever may be said of some of the agencies which precipitate death, death itself is not catching. Yet a contagion of language violently infects the fabric of the verse. Snow is outrageously 'outrageous', night and dawn are indiscriminately 'chopped through'. The language of burial disposes itself as a language of waste: 'I . . . / Threw him down in the hole.' There is the language of inappropriate and indelicate speed: it is a '*quick* prayer' that leads to a satisfied mind. The language even of a quickening realization collapses into the bathetic extraordinary. 'I knew right away he was not . . .'. Not '. . . ordinary'. Or, again, virtue is invested in the bankruptcies of the colloquial and the unredeemedly clichéd:

> she told me that one day we would meet up again,
> And things would be different the next time we wed,
> If I only could hang on and just be her friend.

'Isis' is indeed a tissue of the colloquial and the clichéd: 'where I could not go wrong'; 'somethin' easy to catch'; 'a good price'. The lyric's obsession with the second-handedness of language constitutes an obsession with the way in which the self-conscious self, the self that moves in language, is a collage of the discourses of the culture in which that self is situated. 'I'm in words, made of words, others' words' writes Beckett in *The Unnameable*.[5] In 'Isis' a preoccupation with the sense in which the self-conscious self *is* language forms a preoccupation with the sense in which society and culture are the language which is the self. And the inflexions of the language-uses in 'Isis' are, above all, the inflexions of a materialist culture. The language of possession and exploitation is inalienably a part of the speaker's consciousness. The prospect of something to be gained at no great expense, something easy to catch, is countered immediately with a consideration of finance: 'I got no money.' A man's troth is weighted equal with property: 'I gave him my blanket, he gave me his word.' A body is weighed by its 'price'. 'They tell you "Time is money", as if your life was worth its weight in gold', Dylan was to protest against prevailing ideology in the 1979 lyric 'When You Gonna Wake Up' (*STC*). And in 'Isis' there is not only the overtly brutal materialism of breaking into a tomb in search of the world's biggest necklace. The language of possession conditions the most apparently innocent articulation: 'I could not hold on to her.' Or there is the rapacity of the colloquial response to the poverty of the tomb: 'the casket was empty. / There was no jewels, no nothin', I felt I'd been had.' To have and to hold. Even friendship weighs light against the lack of goods: 'I saw that my partner was just bein' friendly, / When I took up his offer I must-a been mad.'

The self-conscious speaker's desire for Isis is a desire for transcendence of the crude and entrapping language that writes him and is him. An unique and perfect language, an absolute purity of diction, like an ideally civilized state, is banished in this lyric to occupy the same pre-linguistic space as the Other that is sought by the 'I' of the poem. Desire drives a paradoxical protest by the self-conscious self against its own and its culture's degeneracies. Individual identity in 'Isis' is a field of becoming, rather than of being, which witnesses a constant negotiation between contradictory and irreconcilable tendencies. There is a free-play defined in the capacity to protest. But however much desire fuels and celebrates resistance to being written, the struggle for ideal being in the face of the debasements of language also defines identity as a field of pain. There is reaction against even the ideal ground and object of desire. In the eleventh stanza:

> I came in from the East with the sun in my eyes.
> I cursed her one time then I rode on ahead.

A curse at the impossible, maddening predicament of being impelled to catch what cannot be caught. Like the fist of the singer compulsively clenching and unclenching in the film of the live performance at Montreal.[6] 'What drives me to you is what drives me insane.' In the final picture of the lyric, mystical purity – perhaps true lover, perhaps faery child – may beckon with joyful promise of hope or may cruelly mock the melancholy suffering of the human beholder:

> I still can remember the way that you smiled
> On the fifth day of May in the drizzlin' rain.

Speaking the languages of myth and mystic marriage, of psychological nuance, of male adventure, of materialism, 'Isis' at once speaks the language of ordinary human lovers, with all *its* placements and misplacements, its exhaustions, renewals and losses. As Carlos Baker has said of the lovers in so many of Shelley's poems (the 'veiled maid' of 'Alastor', for example, whose voice is 'like the voice' of the 'soul' of the poet who pursues her; or 'Emily' in 'Epipsychidion', addressed by the speaker as 'soul out of my soul'): 'the relationship is … at its highest level, a spiritual union. But it must be, as it were, supported from below by other unifications.'[7] Like 'Isis', Dylan's 1975 'Tangled Up in Blue' (*BT*) also grounds a psychological and metaphysical fable in the commonplaces of earthly lovers' language. In its exploration of a subjectivity that is known and knows itself in language 'Tangled

Up in Blue' employs a linguistic device that may first be considered as it appears in its most basic form in 'I Shall Be Released' (1967; *Biograph*).

'I Shall Be Released' is a work of three stanzas, each of eight lines, the last four lines of each stanza being identical. In the first verse the speaker looks forward to a self-fulfilment. It is to be a fulfilment achieved in despite of the world's easy and limiting opinion that things of value, once lost, can simply be found again or given ready substitutes:

> They say ev'rything can be replaced,
> Yet ev'ry distance is not near.
> So I remember ev'ry face
> Of ev'ry man who put me here.
> I see my light come shining
> From the west unto the east.
> Any day now, any day now,
> I shall be released.

In the second stanza self-realization is again anticipated, and again it is to be achieved despite the circumscribing prescriptions and predictions of others:

> They say ev'ry man needs protection,
> They say ev'ry man must fall.
> Yet I swear I see my reflection
> Some place so high above this wall.
> I see my light come shining...

In the third and final stanza, however, it is not only others that put barriers in the way of self-consummation. In this verse the speaker detaches himself from that part of himself which would seek to deny any responsibility of its own for present frustration.

'Its like Rimbaud said', commented Dylan with reference to his lyric entitled 'Up to Me' (1974; *Biograph*), '"I is another."'[8] In the last stanza of 'I Shall Be Released' another 'I' appears dramatically in the form of another personal pronoun. There is a sudden splitting of persons, with the self-absolving self becoming a 'he':

> Standing next to me in this lonely crowd,
> Is a man who swears he's not to blame.
> All day long I hear him shout so loud,
> Crying out that he was framed.

There is self-criticism in the self-distancing that occurs in these first four lines of the last verse. An acknowledgement that abnegation of self-responsibility can be as important a limiting factor as any externally derived edging or circumscription. One way of setting oneself up for a fall may be to blame others for setting one up.

The antagonism between 'I' and 'they' – the apparently confident affirmation of self against all others – that takes place in the first two stanzas of the lyric is complicated by the dramatic device of the third person pronoun in the third stanza. The splitting of the self into selves, into 'I' and 'he', threatens the secure position of the 'I' that the self-affirmation in the first two stanzas had depended upon. For it is not certain that the 'I' that speaks in the first four lines of the third stanza is directly interchangeable with the 'I' that had spoken in the first two verses. The 'he' that complains 'he was framed' has at least something in common with the 'I' that blames others in the first two stanzas. Perhaps more in common, indeed, than has the 'I' of stanza three who recognizes and stands outside that complaining 'he'. Another 'I' comes into being in this lyric as 'he' is born.

By the end of the lyric it is no longer clear quite who is to be released or from what. Certainly for release read release not only from others but also from other selves. But as far as the latter are concerned there is no certainty about which self may be taken as meriting the privilege of release. When the 'I' that sees its light come shining returns in the closing lines of the last stanza its authority is qualified by such uncertainty. And it is a qualification of authority which underscores the tacit desperation of that 'I''s insistence that freedom is something which lies just around the corner – 'Any day now, any day now':

> I see my light come shining
> From the west unto the east.
> Any day now, any day now,
> I shall be released.

The wish for release in the lyric turns out to be less a wish for release from any particular self than a generalized yearning for a suspension of the fractured, decentred self that is the condition of self-consciousness. But ultimate self-completion, fusion with that perfect self-image projected high above the wall, seems as desirable and temporally unlikely, as transcendental and un-natural, as that the sun should rise and shine from the West.

A play of pronouns comparable to that in 'I Shall Be Released' is often undertaken, with varying degrees of elaboration, by Dylan. 'Tangled Up in Blue' illustrates the way in which such play may take place not only within a single lyric but also between different versions or states of the same lyric.

'Tangled Up in Blue' works apparently with one basic story: in the version performed on *Blood on the Tracks* and printed in *Lyrics, 1962-1985* a first-person speaker tells of a past love affair and of his wanderings following the breakdown of the affair. Within the terms of such a story all the feminine pronouns of the lyric refer to just one person, the lost lover with whom the speaker in the present of the lyric wishes to be reunited. At the opening of the last stanza: 'So now I'm goin' back again, / I got to get to her somehow.' But the play of pronouns in 'Tangled Up in Blue' is inseparable from another characteristic feature of much of Dylan's verse: a duplicity in the exercise of narrative form. In 'Tangled Up in Blue' the narrative is organized less around a simple sequential structure than built up cumulatively by a principle of montage. It is possible to reconstruct from this montage a single, straightforward story. But the disturbance of sequential structure simultaneously gives rise to elements in the text which resist accommodation within such a reconstruction. While the lyric provokes and to some extent satisfies expectations of a straightforward story, it is at the same time actively committed to denying complete fulfilment of those expectations. A preliminary reading attempting to elicit the plainest level of story in the lyric will also provide opportunities to raise some of the problems posed by the text.

In the first four lines of the first stanza the speaker does not merely recall, but recalls recalling his lost love. The next four lines move into the speaker's memories (which might be at once present and past memories) of the attitudes of the family of the lost lover towards their relationship. In the last four lines the speaker remembers himself, apparently alone, preparing for a journey East. It may be inferred that this was a journey undertaken *after* the failure of the love affair. This inference allowed, it remains difficult to fix the chronology more precisely. It might have been a journey taken immediately after the lovers' separation. It might have been taken just after that moment in the past when the speaker remembered his lover. It need not have been taken at either of these moments:

> Early one mornin' the sun was shinin',
> I was layin' in bed

> Wond'rin' if she'd changed at all
> If her hair was still red.
> Her folks they said our lives together
> Sure was gonna be rough
> They never did like Mama's homemade dress
> Papa's bankbook wasn't big enough.
> And I was standin' on the side of the road
> Rain fallin' on my shoes
> Heading out for the East coast
> Lord knows I've paid some dues gettin' through,
> Tangled up in blue.

As a continuing account of the relationship recounted in the first stanza the second stanza would delve a little further back into the past with a mention of the original meeting of the lovers. If the separation that is then described in this verse took place 'out West', the point might link with the speaker's recollection of setting out on a journey East in stanza one:

> She was married when we first met
> Soon to be divorced
> I helped her out of a jam, I guess,
> But I used a little too much force.
> We drove that car as far as we could
> Abandoned it out West
> Split up on a dark sad night
> Both agreeing it was best.
> She turned around to look at me
> As I was walking away
> I heard her say over my shoulder,
> 'We'll meet again someday on the avenue',
> Tangled up in blue.

Stanza three could again be seen to deal with the speaker's travels after the affair was over. But not his travelling East. He would also have journeyed, at some unspecified stage, both North and South:

> I had a job in the great north woods
> Working as a cook for a spell
> But I never did like it all that much
> And one day the ax just fell.
> So I drifted down to New Orleans
> Where I happened to be employed
> Workin' for a while on a fishin' boat
> Right outside of Delacroix.
> But all the while I was alone
> The past was close behind,
> I seen a lot of women
> But she never escaped my mind, and I just grew . . .

In the fourth stanza it is possible to interpret the 'she' that the speaker recalls meeting as once more alluding to the same 'she' as mentioned at the outset of the lyric. Association might also link the woman's prophecy in the second stanza, 'We'll meet again someday . . .', with the event described in this fourth verse:

> She was workin' in a topless place
> And I stopped in for a beer,
> I just kept lookin' at the side of her face
> In the spotlight so clear.
> And later on as the crowd thinned out
> I's just about to do the same,
> She was standing there in back of my chair
> Said to me, 'Don't I know your name?'

> I muttered somethin' underneath my breath,
> She studied the lines on my face.
> I must admit I felt a little uneasy
> When she bent down to tie the laces of my shoe . . .

A chance encounter after the end of the affair with the woman first mentioned in the lyric? A recognition where the speaker judged it best to leave discreetly but where the woman decided to confront the issue? The question 'Don't I know your name?' could suggest just that. Yet the question is also a colloquialism which may serve as an opening line in a meeting between strangers. The question can be taken as a half-ironic expression of recognition or as a humourously forward self-introduction. This latter interpretation of the question is highlighted in an unreleased studio version of the lyric (12 September 1974) where the woman asks, 'Jimmy, what's your name?'[9] Or, again, in the version of the lyric performed at Boston on 21 November 1975 where we find, 'Don't tell me, let me guess your name.'[10] Possibly, then, this might be taken as an account of the very *first* meeting with the woman first mentioned in the lyric.

The episode related in the fifth verse may, though it need not, be understood to follow directly from that narrated in the fourth. At any rate, the woman's expressions in stanza five again move ambiguously between those of an old acquaintance and those of a stranger. The most disconcerting feature in the stanza is the sudden use of the second person in the second to last line:

> She lit a burner on the stove and offered me a pipe
> 'I thought you'd never say hello', she said
> 'You look like the silent type'.
> Then she opened up a book of poems
> And handed it to me
> Written by an Italian poet

> From the thirteenth century.
> And every one of them words rang true
> And glowed like burnin' coal
> Pourin' off of every page
> Like it was written in my soul from me to you,
> Tangled up in blue.

It is a feature that might be construed as a rhetorical direct address by the speaker in the present of the lyric to his lost lover. A way of bearing witness to the continuing significance she, or the memory of her, has for him. But it would remain a disconcerting rupture in the third-person/past tense framework within which she has been contained thus far in the lyric. Is the memorial figure nominated as 'she' at the opening of this stanza to be simply identified with the figure addressed as 'you'? Why initiate this kind of distinction between the two?

Yet more questions are posed by the sixth and penultimate stanza, not least by its sudden introduction of the third-person plural and the masculine third-person singular:

> I lived with them on Montague Street,
> In a basement down the stairs,
> There was music in the cafes at night
> And revolution in the air.
> Then he started into dealing with slaves
> And something inside of him died.
> She had to sell everything she owned
> And froze up inside.
> And when finally the bottom fell out
> I became withdrawn,
> The only thing I knew how to do
> Was to keep on keepin' on like a bird that flew,
> Tangled up in blue.

A reading that aims to construct one story out of the tangled narrative of this lyric might wish to connect this episode with the observation made in the second stanza that 'She was married when we first met.' Literalizing the 'them' and the 'he' in contradistinction to the speaker's 'I' a picture might be constructed of 'he' as the lover's husband and of 'them' as the lover and her husband. But such a view would not offer a particularly clear placing for the speaker's statement that when 'the bottom fell out / I became withdrawn'. If this referred to the end of the woman's relationship with her husband, then the speaker's suggestion of his withdrawal could seem inappropriate to the notion of the development of his own affair with the woman.

Another kind of interpretation recognizes in the distribution of pronouns in the sixth stanza a splitting of perspectives on the self in much the same way as occurs in the splitting of person in 'I Shall Be Released'. In this case the narrator of 'Tangled Up in Blue' would here be viewing his own past self as 'another'. Standing outside and regarding that self as a 'he' the speaker would also stand outside 'them': his past self and his lover of the time. A notable variation on this effect occurs in the September 1974 studio version of 'Tangled Up in Blue' where 'he' displaces 'I' for a large part of the lyric. Thus, in the opening lines:

> Early one mornin' the sun was shinin'
> He was layin' in bed . . .
> Her folks said their lives together . . .
> And he was standin' on the side of the road . . .

In the sixth stanza of this version there is no 'them', only a 'he', a 'she' and an 'I'. In lines six to eight of the stanza a shift from third- to first-person pronoun effects a significant modulation in perspective on the self. At the same time as recognizing in the use of 'he' the alienness of a past self, there is, in the movement into

'I', an allowance that even in the past there was a self that dissociated itself from and critically regarded that other self designated by the 'he':

> He was always in a hurry
> Too busy or too stoned
> And everything that she ever planned
> Just had to be postponed
> She thought they were successful
> He thought they were blessed
> With objects and material things
> But I never was impressed
> And when it all came crashing down
> I became withdrawn
> The only thing I knew how to do
> Was to keep on keepin' on like a bird that flew...

'I was just trying to make it like a painting where you can see the different parts but then you also see the whole of it', commented Dylan on 'Tangled Up in Blue'. '[T]hat's what I was trying to do ... with the concept of time, and the way the characters change from the first person to the third person, and you're never quite sure if the third person is talking or the first person is talking.'[11] Nor, when it comes to the *Blood on the Tracks* and *Lyrics, 1962-1985* version of the lyric, does an identification of 'he' and 'them' as the speaker and his lover in the past help us to be sure of the narrative continuities of the sixth stanza. The ending of a relationship is recorded there. But it is not an ending that necessarily calls to mind the ending already described in stanza two. Then we had heard of a splitting up on a 'dark sad night' following a journey 'West'. In stanza six there is a basement in Montague Street, a change of spirit and then a collapse of relationship suggested in the metaphor of the bottom falling out. None of the details obviously match and it is only the formula of breakdown which is common to both stanzas. The sixth stanza might be taken as offering an amplified account of the same episode as recounted in the second. But the episode of the sixth stanza could just as well be thought of as a different story altogether. Indeed the same point could be made of all the episodes in the lyric.

It is possible to find in 'Tangled Up in Blue' a group of discrete stories oriented around the same basic formula but not necessarily interconnecting at the level of historical detail or event. Looked at this way the lyric would comprise a series of memories of different lovers, recollections of a series of failed relationships. The woman working in the 'topless place' can be literally another than she who was 'married when we first met' and neither is necessarily the same as the woman who had lived in Montague Street. Such an interpretation would solve some of the discontinuities which appear when an attempt is made to understand the lyric as a unified history of the speaker and his one lost love. Taking it this way challenges our expectations of unitary narrative. Our capacity to ground the authority of a story through reference to origins is undermined. No one meeting, no one separation recounted in the lyric, assumes a primary position in relation to another. But we would no longer have to strive to establish connections between the reading of an Italian poet and the living in Montague Street. We would no longer have to struggle to decide whether the episode in the nightclub came before or after the recollection of lost love in stanza one or, say, the separation recollected in stanza two. Yet if such atomization relaxes some of the burdens of response, it fails to exorcise frustration altogether. The single-person 'she', reiterated throughout the lyric, together with the irreducible hints of possible interconnections, perpetually tempt us back into attempting to reconstruct a single story. What is important here is that the lyric successfully hinders any claim to have established certain grounds for preferring one interpretation over the other. Considerable inventive effort on the part of the reader is provoked whether the lyric is taken either as one story or as a series of stories. Co-operation in the making of the story may be demanded of the reader of any narrative. The specially modernist feature of 'Tangled Up in Blue' is that the fragmentation of linear structure, together with the indeterminacy generated by that fragmentation about whether we are in the presence of one or more stories, encourages specific awareness of the creative role of the audience in reading or hearing narrative.

Insistently teasing us into generating story, 'Tangled Up in Blue' also explores the extent to which the mind is fundamentally disposed to think in terms of story or narrative. The conscious self is inseparable from the stories of its own life that it ceaselessly recites, however silently, to itself. It moves in a stream of recountings and recastings of its past thoughts, feelings, situations, actions. It automatically places itself at the end of some plots while positioning itself at various stages of innumerable current plots whose development and ends it can only project or fantasize. In the same way cultures frame themselves through myths of origin, through histories, and through fictions of the future. The self-conscious self, with its memory of things past and its conviction of ends not yet reached, is constituted in narrative. In its disruption of story, 'Tangled Up in Blue' frustrates us into recognition of the conscious self's need to establish terms of reference within coherent episodic patterns, its need to orient itself within this kind of narrative time. The subject of the lyric is in one sense the inescapability of the narrative impulse itself. But more than this, in its disturbance of narrative order the lyric simultaneously inquires into the possibility of something beyond such order.

If, even as one story, the multiple details and events of 'Tangled Up in Blue' are hard to reconcile, and if, as several stories, the one lost lover splinters into several, there is nevertheless a force in the lyric which binds the parts together. It is a force deriving from the lyric's single paradigm of the lost loved one. This paradigm provides a medium – a 'whole' – in which the 'different parts', the disparate details and events of the lyric, are held. It at once inheres in and transcends the literal possibilities of the one or more lovers of the lyric. Haunting the lyric it subsumes the fragments of autobiography or history. The female figure of this paradigm takes on, in relation to the speaker of the lyric, the connotations of a soul mate pursued through the events and substances of the literal world but from whom he is always separated. As a forfeited soul mate she is a spiritual archetype, an ideal pattern of the speaker's own deepest identity. As a figure of a mystical dimension of identity surpassing the boundaries of the self-conscious self, she assumes atemporal possibilities, eluding fixture in narrative detail. It is an atemporality which the shattering of linear continuity in the narrative of the lyric conspires to expose. The order of events recounted in the first six stanzas of the lyric is irrelevant to the archetypal figure of the lost love. The order of those stanzas and the episodes they each enclose could be rearranged, quite arbitrarily, and that figure would remain unaffected. It has to do with 'the break up of time' commented Dylan on the narrative technique of lyrics from *Blood on the Tracks*.[12] Referring to the treatment of time in 'Tangled Up in Blue' he also observed: 'We allow our past to exist. Our credibility is based on our past. But deep in our soul we have no past.'[13] The modification of the third-person/past tense framework by the sudden use of the second person in stanza five marks a notable point in the lyric's attempt to gesture towards an ahistoricity of the soul behind the narrative boundaries of the self. We do not have to seek only literal contiguities between the 'she' that is here locked into the past and the beloved 'you' that is addressed as if present at the time of speaking. It is not so much a memory that is addressed as if it had a living presence as an archetype. And this in the context of words written by 'an Italian poet / From the thirteenth century'. If this is an allusion to Dante it could hardly be more appropriate. Dante the composer of the sonnets of the *Vita Nuova*, where the beloved Beatrice stands as one of the most potent figurative concentrations of a poet-speaker's own spiritual being (not so much an 'autobiography' as an 'autopsychology', as Dante Gabriel Rossetti put it):[14]

> Then she opened up a book of poems
> And handed it to me
> Written by an Italian poet
> From the thirteenth century.
> And every one of them words rang true
> And glowed like burnin' coal
> Pourin' off of every page
> Like it was written in my soul from me to you...

In the last stanza the object of love in 'Tangled Up in Blue' retains its simultaneously literal and archetypal resonance:

> So now I'm goin' back again,
> I got to get to her somehow.
> All the people we used to know
> They're an illusion to me now.
> Some are mathematicians
> Some are carpenter's wives.
> Don't know how it all got started,
> I don't know what they're doin' with their lives.
> But me, I'm still on the road
> Headin' for another joint
> We always did feel the same,
> We just saw it from a different point of view...

Lady Language Creator

The speaker declares that he is going 'back' to find 'her'. This might be understood simply enough as a journey through history to the extent that he intends to find in the present the literal lover of the past, whomsoever she might be. But a little later in the stanza the speaker contrasts the current settledness of old friends ('... carpenter's wives') with his own unfinished, as yet unsatisfied journeying: 'me, I'm still on the road / Headin' for another joint.' Does this failure to pause, to make an end, this continuing movement towards an untravelled world, contradict the opening intention to go *back* again? At a literal level there might be some contradiction here; as if the second statement about journeying away from old association would have to cede priority to the first statement about travelling back to find just such association. But at the level of an archetype that slides beneath history a movement towards an ideal may amount to the same thing as a journeying backwards. Just as a Paradise to be Regained involves the recovery of a Paradise Lost.

The first line of the last stanza in the 1975 Boston concert version of 'Tangled Up in Blue' conflates hints of an equation between forward and backward movements through the addition of a single word: 'So now I'm goin' *on* back again.' It is an addition retained in the much rewritten version of the stanza that Dylan performed in London on 7 July 1984.[15] The *Blood on the Tracks* and *Lyrics, 1962-1985* version of this stanza points obliquely to a common factor beneath the different narratives of the speaker's own life and those of his friends and loved ones ('We always did feel the same, / We just saw it from a different point of view'). But in the 1984 concert version a common spiritual objective beneath such lives emerges explicitly. No longer simply 'it', this objective appears in the form of the archetypal female figure. But here she is situated not only in relation to the speaker. She appears as the object of desire of an unspecific 'We'. It is a 'We' that can embrace not merely the speaker *and* his lover(s) but 'women and men' in general:

> So now I'm goin' on back again
> Maybe tomorrow or maybe next year
> I gotta find someone among the women and men
> Whose destiny is unclear
> Some are masters of illusion
> Some are ministers of the trade
> All of the strong delusion
> All of their beds are unmade
> Me I'm still heading towards the sun
> Trying to stay out of the joint
> We always did love the very same one
> We just saw her from a different point of view
> Tangled up in blue.

Neither speaker nor lyric claims a full apprehension of this 'one'. The self-consciousness of narrative is necessarily estranged from the unselfconscious unity of the soul. In 'Tangled Up in Blue' 'she' is known as out of reach, always to be regained, and yet that knowledge depends on time and narrative. She is herself tangled up in time, tangled up with sadness, in that union with her is precluded by the involvement in time that defines the narratives that speak of her. Her possibility can only be intimated through the interstices of a fractured narrative that, even in its brokenness, cannot transcend time. Dylan's lyric does not so much come to an end as point to an end beyond itself ('still on the road'). For the lyric to reach the end it projects would be a reaching towards its own non-existence. The desire for narrative to end is in an important sense a desire for the ending of narrative, a desire for the stripping away of self-consciousness, a desire for the dissolution of the self ('heading towards the sun'). On the one hand, 'deep in our soul we have no past.' On the other, as Dylan also comments, 'there is a whole lot to reveal beneath the surface of the soul, but it's unthinkable.'[16]

Ultimately unthinkable, uncontainable within narratives of identity, the soul or imagination also knows no sex: 'neither Jew nor Greek ... neither bond nor free ... neither male nor female'.[17] As it subsumes time and the rational self so the imagination subsumes the opposition between masculinity and femininity that is part of language's structuring of reality. The soul may frequently be characterized as feminine – even as Julia Kristeva speaks of the unconscious as 'indifferent to language, enigmatic and feminine' – but in its indifference or anteriority to language this feminine escapes the surface gender specificities of language.[18] In the variant last stanza of the 7 July 1984 performance of 'Tangled Up in Blue' the archetypal 'one' loved by 'We' is cast in terms of the feminine but 'she' moves equally between speaker and lover or between the 'women and men'. And while a feminine characterization is a conventional one the powers of the unconscious may just as readily be spoken of in terms of the masculine – as in the case of Dylan's 'Tambourine Man'. Moving beneath the surface of the self the energies of the soul travel, as we have seen in earlier discussion, beneath syntax, always threatening to undermine the fixed positions of rational and syntactic order. The fluidity of pronoun and person in the versions of 'Tangled Up in Blue' is itself symptomatic of the destabilizing agency of a subliminal power that moves at odds with the order of language as it moves at odds with narrative order. If 'he' replaces 'I' in some versions of 'Tangled Up in Blue', in the opening lines of the 1975 Boston concert version of the lyric the nominal 'I' and 'he' are both displaced by 'she'. Whether 'man' or 'woman' does the remembering, it is all one to the soul:

> Early one mornin' the sun was shinin'
> She was layin' in bed
> Wondrin' if she'd changed at all . . .

If 'Tangled Up in Blue' regrets the entanglements which separate self from soul, another lyric from *Blood on the Tracks*, 'Shelter from the Storm', balances comparable regrets against a delight in the entanglements themselves. Like the speaker of 'Isis' the 'I' of 'Shelter from the Storm' relates a special kind of meeting with 'another'. Throughout the lyric it is a meeting that images a redemption of isolation and alienation, of disorder and depletion. In the first stanza the meeting between self and other is pictured as one that saves the self from its own emptiness:

> 'Twas in another lifetime, one of toil and blood
> When blackness was a virtue and the road was full of mud
> I came in from the wilderness, a creature void of form.
> 'Come in', she said,
> 'I'll give you shelter from the storm'.

This image of respite is simultaneously an image of haven from the fallen world itself. In the eighth stanza, as the speaker questions a putative questioner about the chances of redemption, the image of proffered shelter is juxtaposed with an image of the privations of temporal existence:

> I've heard newborn babies wailin' like a mournin' dove
> And old men with broken teeth stranded without love.
> Do I understand your question, man, is it hopeless and
>   forlorn?
> 'Come in', she said,
> 'I'll give you shelter from the storm'.

Lady Language Creator

Mourning dove: not simply the innocence of the soul that might be confirmed by the *morning* dove (though in performed versions *morning* is punningly heard together with *mourning* and, possibly, *moaning*). Here, even the newborn grieve for something already lost. The elegiac note is proper to the entire lyric. The speaker at the outset of the song tells of an instance in the past when he 'came' in from the wilderness. But whatever home was found, whatever the meeting between self and other, it can never have been more than provisional. For in the present of the lyric the speaker stands separated, debarred from shelter. In the sixth stanza: 'Now there's a wall between us, somethin' there's been lost.'

Nor need the movement from alienation to union to further division be thought of as having happened only once. No more than in 'Tangled Up in Blue' is a single, linear narrative sequence clearly resolved upon in this lyric. A number of verses turn around the same paradigm, but they do not all tell the same story. The coming in from privation recorded in the first stanza, though comparable in structure, is not necessarily historically the same event as the instances we are told about in, say, stanzas three and five:

> Not a word was spoke between us, there was little risk involved
> Everything up to that point had been left unresolved.
> Try imagining a place where its always safe and warm.
> 'Come in', she said,
> 'I'll give you shelter from the storm'.

> Suddenly I turned around and she was standin' there
> With silver bracelets on her wrists and flowers in her hair.
> She walked up to me so gracefully and took my crown of thorns.
> 'Come in', she said,
> 'I'll give you shelter from the storm'.

Lady Language Creator

The meetings in 'Shelter from the Storm' envisage respite from suffering and healing of fragmentation; respite and healing that are caught in the reciprocities of self and other that characterize the refrain, where the 'I' of the speaker of the verses becomes a 'you' to the 'she' who in turn is translated into a speaking 'I'. But reciprocity is not integration. As the speaker records his continuing separation from the 'she', so even the insistent repetition of that other's offer of shelter defines a presence continually re-apprehended, never finally possessed.

In 'Shelter from the Storm', as in 'Isis', the alternation between exile and home is bound to a principle of repetition. Failure effects a removal to the wilderness, while removal fires a return drive homeward. Each alienation is new and already known: 'I rode straightaway for the wild unknown country where I could not go wrong.' Each return is a predictable renewal. In the last verse of 'Shelter from the Storm': 'Well, I'm living in a foreign country, but I'm bound to cross the line.' A final crossing, an erasure of the lines of distinction and difference, lies beyond the terms of this lyric. For the bourne recurrently represented, never finally occupied, is in its ultimate sense one from which no traveller returns. This shelter images a union of self with archetype that lies outside language and time. It is an image of that undivided state the loss of which is immediately mourned by the newly differentiated human subject, the wailing of the new born babe. It is an untraceable origin or a Beauty foregone, forever desired, evermore about to be, irrecoverable this side of language and time:

> I'm living in a foreign country but I'm bound to cross the line
> Beauty walks a razor's edge, someday I'll make it mine.
> If I could only turn back the clock to when God and her were born.

Lady Language Creator

'Come in', she said,
'I'll give you shelter from the storm'.

A Beauty that walks a razor's edge is a Beauty that transcends division. A Beauty not associated *either* with pleasure *or* with pain. It is both and neither. Like the cutting pleasure of the image itself. And yet the apprehension of such Beauty is dependent upon the discriminations of self-consciousness, upon the painful gratification of knowing of a condition the attainment of which is denied by the knowing. And for all the visions of human hurt in 'Shelter from the Storm', for all the doubts ('is it hopeless and forlorn'), the lyric also celebrates the division that is the condition of a knowledge of Beauty. In stanza four there is less elegaic grieving than comic delight in the accumulation of images of waste and persecution:

I was burned out from exhaustion, buried in the hail,
Poisoned in the bushes an' blown out on the trail,
Hunted like a crocodile, ravaged in the corn.

An exuberance underwriting these lines surfaces in the wryly humorous deal offered by the second line of the ninth stanza, as the speaker recalls his treatment at the hands of the world:

In a little hilltop village, they gambled for my clothes
I bargained for salvation an' they gave me a lethal dose.
I offered up my innocence and got repaid with scorn.

The blasphemy of these lines touches the same note of self-irony as that sounded in the fifth stanza when 'She walked up to me so gracefully and took my crown of thorns.' At the same time as we are asked to take seriously the lyric's images of alienation, we are also invited to witness the speaker's self-mocking awareness of the pretension of his role as a type of suffering humanity.

The plurality of tone and perspective in the lyric extends directly to the imagining of relief from turmoil. In the third stanza the shelter can take on oppressively claustrophobic, regressively stifling possibilities. There may be here, as whenever the offer is reiterated, something insinuatingly threatening at the heart of the promised good:

> Try imagining a place where it's always safe and warm.
> 'Come in', she said,
> 'I'll give you shelter from the storm'.

It is to Dylan's representation of disturbing possibilities within the very places that might be thought to offer shelter that we may now turn. The next chapter begins by examining further the kind of anxiety that is evident in Dylan's work concerning a notion of the self as bound up in language and narrative. As we have seen in the discussions of the preceding chapters, such anxieties are frequently counterbalanced in Dylan by an emphasis on the positive potential of energies that are uncontained by the cultural and the contingent. At crucial points, however, Dylan's work finds in those energies less a restorative force than a baleful power.

5
That Enemy Within

> I see the screws breaking loose, see the devil pounding on tin,
> I see a house in the country being torn from within.
> I can hear my ancestors calling from the land far beyond.
>   'Caribbean Wind' (1980; *Biograph*)

'Oh if there's an original thought out there, I could use it right now.' So says the speaker of 'Brownsville Girl', from the 1986 album *Knocked Out Loaded*, in a line which reflects upon one of the fundamental preoccupations of the lyric.[1] This seventeen stanza work, co-written by Dylan with playwright Sam Shepard, opens with a speaker remembering a film that he once saw.[2] In the first two stanzas, the stock diction and conventions of a Western compose the memory:

> Well, there was this movie I seen one time,
> About a man riding 'cross the desert and it starred Gregory
> Peck.
> He was shot down by a hungry kid try'n' to make a name
> for himself.
> The townspeople wanted to crush that kid down and
> string him up by the neck.

That Enemy Within

> Well the Marshall, now he beat that kid to a bloody pulp
> As the dying gunfighter lay in the sun and gasped for his last breath.
> Turn him loose, let him go, let him say he outdrew me fair and square,
> I want him to feel what it's like to every moment face his death.

It is when the crescendo of cliché has been reached in the last line of the second verse – with its stereotype of manliness at the outlawed edge of experience – that the recollections momentarily break and the speaker expresses his disdain for the formulae purveyed by the film. But disdain is accompanied by a recognition that such formulae are, inescapably, a part of the raw material of memory and mind. At the beginning of the third verse:

> Well I keep seeing this stuff and it just comes a-rolling in
> And you know it blows right through me like a ball and chain

The speaker shifts abruptly in the remaining two lines of the third verse into 'speaking internally'[3] to a figure whose present reality for him is, like the film, a memorial one: 'You know I can't believe we've lived so long and are still so far apart / The memory of you keeps callin' after me like a rollin' train.' From this point onwards the lyric weaves in and out of different strains of the speaker's mind. And one of the difficulties presented by the lyric is that it is impossible to identify with certainty a position from which the speaker is speaking. Towards the end, in the fourteenth stanza, we come as close as we are allowed to establishing such a position: 'Well, I'm standin' in line in the rain to see a movie starring Gregory Peck.' Hence, perhaps, the reminiscence of the Peck film at the opening of the lyric. But, we are told of the film about to be seen, 'you know it's not the one that I had in mind.' *Had* in mind, not *have* in mind. The present of the fourteenth stanza insists at least on a temporal distance from the start of the lyric's own succession. There is, moreover, another present in the sixth verse of the lyric which situates the speaker in a quite different location from that of the film queue. Stanzas four and five relate a past meeting and a journey with a woman who is apparently the one addressed and remembered in the closing two lines of the third verse. At the opening of the fourth stanza: 'I can still see the day that you came to me on the painted desert'; and in the fifth: '. . . we drove that car all night into San Anton / And we slept near the Alamo, your skin was so tender and soft.' But the sixth verse not only introduces another car and another woman. It speaks, suddenly, in the present tense: 'Well, we're drivin' this car and the sun is comin' up over the Rockies, / Now I know she ain't you but she's here and she's got that dark rhythm in her soul.' The passage can in fact be read as another memory – the memory of an occasion and a person standing, say, to the speaker waiting in the queue, in a less distant past than the woman and the events alluded to in the third, fourth and fifth stanzas. It would be a past that is vitally 'present' to the speaker's consciousness and which is momentarily reinhabited appropriately in the present tense. Following the sixth stanza the lyric returns to the past tense and to recountings of more situations and journeys once undertaken, which may at points be memories of the past that was shared with the woman first mentioned in the third stanza. But as episode gives way to new episode, and as recurring episodes are intertwined with further recollections of the film mentioned at the outset of the lyric, fixed points of view and clear narrative frames of reference are never resolved.

Throughout 'Brownsville Girl' scraps of memory and thought mix with other scraps in an unstable temporal sequence. The lyric plays with tenses and perspectives as it enacts the lack of chronological structure in the inner life of the mind. Successive displacements of thoughts and memories lend a phantasmagoric dimension to the movements of consciousness traced in the verses. But it is not only that the lyric invokes a technique representing a 'stream of consciousness ... going backwards and forwards in time' without 'any grossly discernible beginning or middle or end'.[4] It is not only the fluidity of memory or mind which the lyric dips into. It is that throughout 'Brownsville Girl' the mind's images and memories have only a questionably 'real' status.

The first hint of such questionableness comes in stanzas four and five. 'I can still see the day that you came to me on the painted desert', says the speaker in stanza four, 'I could never figure out why you chose that particular place to meet / Ah, but you were right. It was perfect as I got in behind the wheel.' In stanza five: 'Well we drove that car all night into San Anton' ...' A perfect place to meet and from which to embark on a night's journey. But it is a perfection that is questionable in its aesthetic resonance. The apparent reference to the Painted Desert of Arizona bears an ironic connotation of artifice, a hint of the state of a film set: 'the *painted* desert'. The drive down to San Anton' is oddly coloured by an insinuation of its origin in some order of fiction. From this stage onwards 'Brownsville Girl' explores, in a variety of ways, a collapsing of distinction between actual or real and artificial or fictional. Stanza ten, for example, marks one of the occasions when the speaker returns to the matter of the Gregory Peck film mentioned at the start of the lyric. But in this recollection no separation is maintained between a self that once watched a film and the film itself. A story of self becomes confused with the narrative that composes a memory of that self: 'Something about that movie though, well I just can't get it out of my head / But I can't remember why I was in it or what part I was supposed to play.' In its exploration of memory, 'Brownsville Girl' is preoccupied with the question of whether it is ever possible to isolate

That Enemy Within

a 'true' or 'real' self from the cultural context within which that self takes shape. For all practical purposes it may be easy enough to separate a sense of self from a viewing of a Gregory Peck Western. But the question put by the lyric is whether the Peck film is not just a particular manifestation of underlying models of reality and identity offered by a culture at large. Models that are not discernible simply in a culture's explicit fictions, but which govern the constitution of individual identity within that culture. So that a self's conception of itself and of its experience may manifest the same paradigms as a film which that self sees or a book which it reads.

In 'Brownsville Girl' the speaker's recollections of his past – of the history of his 'real' life as against the narrative of a film which he once saw – turn out to be themselves composed of the recognizable formulae of American cultural representation; particularly, though not exclusively, filmic representation. There is throughout the lyric the dominant motif of movement and journey; a motif which, in the episode recollected in the seventh stanza, momentarily settles at the end of the third line into a familiar icon. 'We pulled up where Henry Porter used to live', we are told in the second line, and in the third, 'Ruby was in the backyard hanging clothes, she had her red hair tied back. She saw us come rolling up in a trail of dust'. Disillusionment in the American dream of fulfilment is itself a stock theme of American art and the speaker's recollections here reconstitute the theme in its most tired aspect. It is an exhaustion highlighted in the echoing of 'B' movie titles (*Night of the Living Dead* or, perhaps, *The Return of the Living Dead*)[5] in the speech of the woman remembered by the speaker:

> [Ruby] told us how times were tough and about how she
>   was thinkin' of bummin' a ride back to from where she
>   started.

75

> But ya know, she changed the subject every time money
> came up.
> She said, 'Welcome to the land of the living dead'. You
> could tell she was so broken-hearted.

Yet the suffering that is the subject of the cliché is itself sharpened by the tacit recognition of the given nature of individual patterns of experience. A similar tonal complexity – balancing contempt at the predetermined aspect of themes of individual development against an admission of the travail that may accompany definition within such themes – emerges in the ninth stanza. Here, a version of the inherited dream of endless movement Westwards, a fantasy of travelling to the outermost limits of experience, is parodied in the bathetic projection of extremes in the second and third lines:

> 'How far are y'all going?' Ruby asked us with a sigh.
> 'We're going all the way 'till the wheels fall off and burn,
> 'Till the sun peels the paint and the seat covers fade and
> the water moccasin dies'.

But however predictably reiterated such stories of the self may be, the burdens of entrapment are not the less heavy for those innocently constructed within the fiction:

> Ruby just smiled and said, 'Ah, you know some babies
> never learn'.

Again, in the case of the episode suddenly introduced in the eleventh and twelfth stanzas, it is impossible to determine the limits of the real as against those of the fictional. The event fragmentarily recalled by the speaker in the eleventh verse has the ring of a particular kind of melodrama. It is a melodrama

That Enemy Within

accented in the performance of the lyric on *Knocked Out Loaded* as the chorus utters a mocking, parodic murmur at the phrase 'when shots rang out':

> Well, they were looking for somebody with a pompadour.
> I was crossin' the street when shots rang out.
> I didn't know whether to duck or to run, so I ran.

In the twelfth stanza, which does nothing further to place this episode in either an actual or an imagined zone, the confusion of the real and the artificial in the speaker's being is endorsed by the mysterious assertion of the last two lines:

> Well, you saw my picture in the Corpus Christi Tribune.
>   Underneath it, it said, 'A man with no alibi'.
> You went out on a limb to testify for me you said I was
>   with you.
> Then when I saw you break down in front of the judge
>   and cry real tears,
> It was the best acting I saw anybody do.

'"A man with no alibi."' The phrase talismanically formulates the speaker's sense of being unable to prove a real presence for the self outside all shows of reality. Second-handedness seems the inevitable condition of utterance in 'Brownsville Girl'. The slick inflexions of, say, a Chandleresque fiction infect even the speaker's reflection in the fifteenth stanza:

> You know, it's funny how things never turn out the way
>   you had 'em planned.
> The only thing we knew for sure about Henry Porter is
>   that his name wasn't Henry Porter.

> And you know there was somethin' about you baby that I
>   liked that was always too good for this world
> Just like you always said there was somethin' about me
>   you liked that I left behind in the French Quarter.

It is hardly surprising that in the thirteenth verse the speaker should declare: 'Oh if there's an original thought out there, I could use it right now.' But the irony of this line is that it is forces 'out there' which deprive the speaker of originality.

And yet 'Brownsville Girl', for all its parodies and ironies, indeed by virtue of its parodies and ironies, implies the possibility of a position from which the contingency of the self may be measured. Implied throughout, and not least in the register of distress at the thought of second-handedness, is a space for identity which can stand free of the ball and chain. It is an implication endorsed in the performance of the lyric when in the seventeenth stanza the chorus cries 'Oh no' to the speaker's statement that, while he can remember seeing the Gregory Peck film, 'I don't remember who I was or where I was bound.' It is an implication again echoed in the performance of the lyric when at the end of the sixteenth stanza the chorus utters a strangulated scream after the words '"let's hope that the roof stays on."' A kind of sub-verbal protest at the articulation of the self by external convention, it is a wail that asserts a heart's anguish and, in that anguish, some ground of autonomy:

> You always said people don't do what they believe in,
>   they just do what's most convenient, then they repent.
> And I always said, 'Hang on to me, baby, and let's hope
>   that the roof stays on'.

A claim that the self may be bound even at the moment it is speaking up for freedom had formed the substance of Dylan's

That Enemy Within

protest, in the 1964 'My Back Pages' (*Another Side of Bob Dylan*), at some of his own political verses of the early 1960s. Not that this lyric insists that social and political engagement must be avoided, but rather that guard needs be kept against the fatal falsities of an easy idealism: 'Lies that life is black and white / Spoke from my skull.' Words that violently speak against violence may find themselves only pawns in the game of violence: '"Rip down all hate", I screamed.' The self that writes itself in preceptive opposition to precept may find that it has in fact been written according to the rules it would oppose:

> In a soldier's stance, I aimed my hand
> At the mongrel dogs who teach
> Fearing not that I'd become my enemy
> In the instant that I preach

Like 'Brownsville Girl', however, 'My Back Pages' reserves a right to unwrite those scripts of the self that seem most entrapping. And numerous Dylan lyrics unreservedly affirm the exfoliating energies of personality: energies of the psyche that can radically throw over limiting structures of the self, whether those structures are thought of as received ones or even as the now inert forms – the socially recuperated forms – of once original expressions of personality. In 'It's All Over Now, Baby Blue' (*BABH*), for example, the order under which the addressee of the lyric currently lives ('*This* sky') is seen as losing viability:

> The empty-handed painter from your streets
> Is drawing crazy patterns on your sheets.
> This sky, too, is folding under you
> And it's all over now, Baby Blue.

'I held it truth', wrote Tennyson, 'That men may rise on stepping-stones / Of their dead selves. ...' A metaphor of individual development recalling that in section I of *In Memoriam* is not only doubted but invoked and dismissed in 'It's All Over Now, Baby Blue'. The lyric envisages a drama in which one pulsion of identity is engaged in disordering nominal certainties of self. The voice of the lyric, recognizing the inevitability of the disordering while acknowledging the pull of faint-heartedness, incites Baby Blue to respond to a call away from the safely plotted course, away from constricting definition by extinct modes of being:

> Leave your stepping stones behind, something calls for you.
> Forget the dead you've left, they will not follow you.

And if, in this lyric, dead selves do not rise, neither do their offspring, their productions, retain a living relation with a progenitor. The creative self is no longer intimate with those productions. And they suffer a bereftness and a loss of efficacy as of a fire neutralized in the heat of the sun. A bereftness and an impotence that are unaltered for all that they may be bitterly regretted:

> Yonder stands your orphan with his gun,
> Crying like a fire in the sun.

Baby Blue is asked in this lyric to re-embrace a lack of fixture which has been forfeited through a fossilization of attitudes and roles. It is an appeal to re-identify with a principle of identity that refuses settlement and control. It is time for another fire to be started in place of the one which has been defused. The vagabond who emblematizes the call of this principle is one of the troupe of irregular and carnivalesque figures that processes through Dylan's work:

> The vagabond who's rapping at your door
> Is standing in the clothes that you once wore.
> Strike another match, go start anew
> And it's all over now, Baby Blue.

Like the empty-handed painter whose street-surrealism unsettles the domestic composure of Baby Blue's sheets, the vagabond is a relation not only of Tambourine Man, of ragged clown, or of Isis herself, but of the 'mystery tramp' of 'Like a Rolling Stone', characterized by the 'vacuum of his eyes'. And as with 'Like a Rolling Stone', 'Mr. Tambourine Man', or 'Isis', there is something disconcerting about the usurpation of the known in 'It's All Over Now, Baby Blue'. But again, as with such lyrics, 'It's All Over Now, Baby Blue' tends to emphasize the creative and positive potential of abandonment to spaces of unmapped, unwritten possibility.

The same emphasis is not always to be found in Dylan's lyrics. Not in 'Desolation Row' (*H61*), for instance. The first nine of the ten stanzas of this work orchestrate a series of variations on the theme of the modern world as waste land. It is, in the eighth stanza, a benighted world, where power presides through a sinister indirection and whose presiding powers are directed by ignorance. Its working routines deal in death ('heart-attack machine') and its hierarchy ('castles') in both specious brotherhood ('insurance men') and branding intimidation ('kerosene'):

> Now at midnight all the agents
> And the superhuman crew
> Come out and round up everyone
> That knows more than they do
> Then they bring them to the factory
> Where the heart attack machine
> Is strapped across their shoulders

> And then the kerosene
> Is brought down from the castles
> By insurance men . . .

In pursuit of its theme 'Desolation Row' recontextualizes – within a modern urban scene – a variety of figures from Western literature, folklore and history. It is via Shakespeare, for example, that in the fourth stanza we hear of the spiritual sterility – amounting to a kind of dementia – induced by the values and practices of secular, mechanistic civilization:

> Now Ophelia, she's 'neath the window
> For her I feel so afraid
> On her twenty-second birthday
> She already is an old maid
> To her, death is quite romantic
> She wears an iron vest
> Her profession's her religion
> Her sin is her lifelessness

But the lyric's casting of the inhabitants of the modern world in terms of well-known Western figures and types does not guarantee an affirmation of cultural continuity. At the end of the second stanza, it is not only that Cinderella's disinheritance and drudgery are re-imagined within the violence of the contemporary city. One of the issues raised is whether, in being so relocated, she is dispossessed of – orphaned from – the happy fairy-tale outcome of her original story:

> the only sound that's left
> After the ambulances go
> Is Cinderella sweeping up
> On Desolation Row

That Enemy Within

Comparably, in the fifth stanza, Einstein is displaced from a familiar legend of his life's work. In this stanza the oppression of modern Western culture lies not so much in its capacity to exclude as in its will to include: in its anaesthetizing accommodation of contrasts. A monk here is jealous of Einstein yet fraternizes with him as a friend. The vitality of the disjunction between a traditional religious world view, with its conception of absolutes, and an insurgent scientific, relativistic ideology, is denied. Einstein and *his* false brother the monk participate in a cultural symbiosis which debases even the distinction between love and hate. Removed from his place in a legend of radical theoretical difference Einstein can only pretend to be an outlaw, condemned to the harmless iteration of an approved non-conformity:

>Einstein, disguised as Robin Hood
>With his memories in a trunk
>Passed this way an hour ago
>With his friend, a jealous monk
>He looked so immaculately frightful
>As he bummed a cigarette
>Then he went off sniffing drainpipes
>And reciting the alphabet

In the seventh stanza, 'The Phantom of the Opera' appears in 'A perfect image of a priest', a conjunction which sharply images a spiritually disfigured society. The same stanza goes on to witness a disfiguring of the story of Casanova. Here again a threat is contained by assimilation. In the culture of 'Desolation Row' sexual promiscuity is licensed in order that its subversive power be spent:

>They're spoonfeeding Casanova
>To get him to feel more assured

83

> Then they'll kill him with self-confidence
> After poisoning him with words

To lose the self through being spoonfed with self. The destructive power of a culture in which anything goes, in which all fables of self are generously tolerated, is captured in the dislocations of story perpetrated in the lyric. Cut off from the integrity of their familiar stories, such characters as Casanova are cut off from their own identities. 'Desolation Row' deals in images of the enclosure of discrete parts of the body. Ophelia 'wears an iron vest'. But there is not only an imagery of mechanical disjunction and entrapment; of being, as it were, locked within a fragmented self. There is also a motif of being locked out of the self. Einstein stands outside his own mind as he stands outside his own recognizable narrative: 'Einstein, disguised as Robin Hood / With his memories in a trunk'.

A crucial image of the devaluation of fables of identity within the wasted and wasting culture of 'Desolation Row' occurs in the lyric's third stanza. In this verse an unreliableness at the root of official appearance is suggested by a Good Samaritan who is distinguished by an attention to his own costume rather than by his concern, as in the Gospel story, for another who has been 'stripped ... of his raiment'.[6]

> the Good Samaritan, he's dressing
> He's getting ready for the show
> He's going to the carnival tonight
> On Desolation Row

What is important here, and throughout the lyric, is that the forces of alienation are indistinguishable from the forces of carnival. It is, specifically, a carnivalesque disorder which saturates approved pattern in 'Desolation Row'. And what is most

That Enemy Within

striking is that that disorder does not bear, as so often in Dylan, a creative aspect. It is itself the source of the negativity which constitutes the waste land. The darkness of unreason which overwhelms all structures and forms in 'Desolation Row' defines no redemptive possibility but only an obscure malignity. The lyric's opening lines present, through a series of absurdist vignettes, a culture's profound confusion of terms:

> They're selling postcards of the hanging
> They're painting the passports brown
> The beauty parlor is filled with sailors
> The circus is in town

In the succeeding lines, the circus comes to image a principle of perversion entering social forms but exceeding and mocking any formulation of social authority and control:

> Here comes the blind commissioner
> They've got him in a trance
> One hand is tied to the tight-rope walker
> The other is in his pants

The troubled energies of 'Desolation Row' threaten to annihilate the culture they negatively inspire. As one commentator has noted, 'Desolation Row' confronts us 'with recurring hints of imminent disaster'.[7] The tension instinct in the commissioner's delusory holding of balance is confirmed in the image of latent violence – an image reversing official readings of the relationship between order and disorder – offered in the concluding lines of the first stanza:

> And the riot squad they're restless
> They need somewhere to go

85

> As Lady and I look out tonight
> From Desolation Row

There is an insinuation of the coming end of all fortunes as, in the third stanza, the firmament itself retires and the teller of fortunes withdraws from business:

> Now the moon is almost hidden
> The stars are beginning to hide
> The fortunetelling lady
> Has even taken all her things inside

Ominous hints of the penalty of the fall – the allusion in the third stanza to Cain and Abel, who are left on the street after the fortunetelling lady has retreated, or to Ophelia's gazing upon 'Noah's great Rainbow' in the fourth stanza – heighten the correlation sustained throughout the lyric between the gathering madness of the carnival and the inexorable onset of evening and darkness.

But it is the opening lines of the penultimate stanza that provide the most notable single 'evocation of impending catastrophe':[8]

> Praise be to Nero's Neptune
> The Titanic sails at dawn

Thus modern Western culture is imaged as a ship of fools about to go down. Two images of dangerous unreason are conflated here. In the first place this culture is likened to the Titanic as the ship of fools who continued to play and dance even as they were sinking. Secondly, the Neptune that belonged to the careless passengers on the Titanic belongs also to Nero, who fiddled while Rome burned. The end of an unregenerate culture is about to come in an apocalyptic conflux – realizing the potential of kerosene as an inflammable liquid – of fire and water.

Yet the bleakest element of 'Desolation Row' is that the lyric floats the possibility of a detached, saving perspective on disturbance only to overturn that possibility. Desolation Row itself is, at one level in the lyric, a name for the space where chaos happens and where people are deserted. At the same time, however, the Row stands in the lyric for an outlook that perceives the incoherence. Thus it is that 'Lady and I' in the first stanza look out on a mad world '*From* Desolation Row'. In this sense the Row, as a perspective of the mind, might constitute some kind of refuge from insanity. In the eighth stanza, indeed, the powers of oppression seek to prevent escape not *from* but *to* Desolation Row:

> insurance men who go
> Check to see that nobody is escaping
> To Desolation Row

As a position of the mind the Row and its insights are evaded by a culture that is rooted in an absurd that bears no regenerative potential. In the penultimate stanza it is an absurdity that already spells, were it but known, an annihilation by flood, a watery death such as has been intimated since the ironic reference to rain in the third stanza ('Everybody is making love / Or else expecting rain'), or since the reference in the fourth verse to Ophelia and the assumed story of her death by water:

> The Titanic sails at dawn
> And everybody's shouting
> 'Which side are you on?'
> And Ezra Pound and T. S. Eliot
> Fighting in the captain's tower

> While calypso singers laugh at them
> And fishermen hold flowers
> Between the windows of the sea
> Where lovely mermaids flow
> And nobody has to think too much
> About Desolation Row

In the very last stanza the voice of the lyric alters stance and speaks as if addressing a personal acquaintance who is failing to grasp the crippled ('lame') and crippling nature of the carnival. The image of the unopenable door in the second line suggests that there is no passage back to careless involvement in the carnival once certain insights have been gained:

> Yes, I received your letter yesterday
> (About the time the doorknob broke)
>   .   .   .   .   .
> All these people that you mention
> Yes, I know them, they're quite lame
> I had to rearrange their faces
> And give them all another name
> Right now I can't read too good
> Don't send me no more letters no
> Not unless you mail them
> From Desolation Row

But occupancy of Desolation Row as a position from which the chaos can be viewed does not emancipate the viewer from horror. The rearrangement of faces and names mentioned in the last stanza describes metafictionally the poetic procedures – the tamperings with character and story – of the preceding nine stanzas themselves. Those tamperings constitute a rewriting of the received forms of stories in an attempt to demonstrate the essential incoherence of the culture that lives by such stories. The speaker in the last stanza insists on an inability to read the received narratives and asserts that only rewritten versions – versions scripted, like those of this lyric, from desolation's perspective – are acceptable. But the desolating double-bind explored by this lyric is that the rearrangement – the felt necessity to rewrite – can itself stand as a manifestation of the ill pervading the culture rather than a revolutionary act which transcends that ill. The act of fracturing and redistributing – disturbing the surface patterns of approved culture – is indistinguishable in the lyric from the inherent disorder which the act of disturbance sets out to expose. 'These fragments I have shored against my ruins' observes a voice towards the end of T. S. Eliot's *The Wasteland*. The poetic practices of 'Desolation Row' owe a debt to the work of such as T. S. Eliot. Yet even as the lyric pursues that inheritance it is conscious too of the possible fruitlessness of assuming that ruin may be fought with or healed by ruin. The modernist experiment in disruption emerges in this Dylan lyric as another manifestation of a world shattered inside and out: a manifestation which has no separate status from and no renovative purchase on that world:

> Ezra Pound and T. S. Eliot
> Fighting in the captain's tower
> While calypso singers laugh at them ...

'Desolation Row' embraces the Pyrrhicism of its own victory in refusing the illusion of order. The refuge on one side of the door with the broken knob is not free of the disturbed and disturbing valencies which characterize the other side of the door. It may define an insight that is lacking on the blind side but destruction threatens alike those who are carelessly or carefully driven by the energies of the carnival. The problem is subtly anticipated in the

That Enemy Within

fourth stanza. Here Ophelia is described as looking, in conformity with authorized fables of potential redemption, for a sign of deliverance from death by water. She fixes hopes upon the sign that in Genesis (9:13-17) indicates both the abatement of the flood sent to purge human kind and the beginning of a new Covenant between God and humanity. But whatever the convention that directs her so to look, she is drawn nevertheless to an alternative wisdom that is associated with the perspective from Desolation Row:

> Her sin is her lifelessness
> And though her eyes are fixed upon
> Noah's great rainbow
> She spends her time peeking
> Into Desolation Row

The articulation of a wisdom that does not innoculate against the danger of which the wisdom speaks contitutes a whole other side to Dylan's lyrical treatment of potencies that lie beyond common sense. It is an articulation that is often intimate with the apocalyptic tenor of many Dylan lyrics. As early as the 1963 'A Hard Rain's A-Gonna Fall' (*The Freewheelin' Bob Dylan*) the knowledge that the rain will fall does not simply exempt the visionary from submergence:

> I'm a-goin back out 'fore the rain starts a-fallin',
> I'll walk to the depths of the deepest black forest,
> Where the people are many and their hands are all empty,
> Where the pellets of poison are flooding their waters,
> . . . . .
> And I'll tell it and think it and speak it and breath it,
> And reflect it from the mountain so all souls can see it,
> Then I'll stand on the ocean until I start sinkin' . . .

That Enemy Within

Comparably, 'Desolation Row' identifies no ground to survive the deluge. If Noah's rainbow is hardly believed in, the dawn which the lyric does look foward to is a false one: 'The Titanic sails at dawn'. Desolation Row, *either* as the space where chaos happens *or* as the perspective from which the chaos is grasped, is a desolate place. And it is that place - not some newly covenanted order - that the lyric itself comes to rest in. Unlike the modernist voices of many of Dylan's lyrics the modernist voice of 'Desolation Row' speaks of a crippled condition as a cripple.

The negativity of the energies at play in 'Desolation Row' and the speaker's own implication in that negativity find a parallel - within a narrower focus - in another of Dylan's lyrics to examine the nature of the imaginative principle informing artistic creation. In 'She Belongs to Me' (*BABH*) the darker aspect of daemonic energy - hinted at but not dwelt upon in lyrics such as 'Mr. Tambourine Man' or 'Eternal Circle' - comes markedly to the fore. The first stanza of 'She Belongs to Me' emphasizes the autonomy of the imagination - figured as anima - and sketches its capacity to invert and transvalue the divisions and oppositions upon which the rational self and its world are predicated:

> She's got everything she needs,
> She's an artist, she don't look back.
> She can take the dark out of the nighttime
> And paint the daytime black.

The third verse stresses the transcendent scope of imaginative resource, its lack of filiation and its transgressive power:

> She never stumbles,
> She's got no place to fall.
> She's nobody's child
> The Law can't touch her at all.

That Enemy Within

To the extent that such a power may be ritually contained, any mortal feast-day will serve the purpose:

> Bow down to her on Sunday,
> Salute her when her birthday comes.
> For Halloween give her a trumpet
> And for Christmas, buy her a drum.

Hallowe'en, of course, may from one point of view be the Eve of All Saints, but from another it is the night of all the witches. And in this lyric, to bow down to 'nobody's child', one who does not really have a day of birth, turns out to be not only a matter of worship but of being spellbound by a dangerous and dessicating power:

> She wears an Egyptian ring
> That sparkles before she speaks.
> She's a hypnotist collector,
> You are a walking antique.

The local transgressions incited by the imagination's transcendence turn out to be performed in thrall of a cruel and disabling authority:

> You will start out standing
> Proud to steal her anything she sees.
> But you will wind up peeking through her keyhole
> Down upon your knees.

The irony of the lyric's title is founded in recognition that the imagination is not owned by the ordinary self: 'She' does not belong to 'me', but the other way around.

Thraldom to menacing potencies of the psyche that draw their

That Enemy Within

power from without the socialized self is again the subject of the 1978 'New Pony' (*SL*). The image of the horse in this lyric is at one level a figure of the inner drive and life of the psyche. It is indeed a type of anima-figure. But it is the anima in its direst aspect. No elusive spirit, she appears here as a token of primal instinctive energy. And the opening line of the lyric baldly associates this energy with a fallen principle: 'Once I had a pony, her name was Lucifer.' Not that the lyric asserts that this principle has been exorcized. The 'new pony' of the lyric's title is a reincarnation of the old one. In the third stanza, beneath whatever formal refinements that are affected by the new pony, reside not merely libidinal force but satyric, diabolic features:

I got a new pony, she knows how to fox-trot, lope and pace
. . . .
She got great big hind legs
And long black shaggy hair above her face.

The images of old and new ponies in 'New Pony' are images of the presence and unavoidable resurgence of a noxious power within the self. And when in the fourth stanza the speaker shifts into addressing directly his own other, darkest self, he is addressing not only the peccant force represented by the new pony, but the satanic principle first figured in terms of the pony named Lucifer. For Lucifer both as the morning star and the archangel fallen from light is at the heart of this self-reflexive address:

It was early in the mornin', I seen your shadow in the door
Now, I don't have to ask nobody
I know what you come here for

Continuing this address in the fifth verse the speaker registers the unmanageable compulsions of his own shadowy self and perceives the threat to himself and others posed by those compulsions:

> They say you're usin' voodoo, I seen your feet walk by themselves
> Oh, baby, that god you been prayin' to
> Is gonna give ya back what you're wishin' on someone else

But while old and new ponies serve at one level as figures of the speaker's own unregenerate nature, they at once define the objects of attack – specifically sexual victims – of that nature. And, in this sense, they are not only victims of the speaker. For they too are driven by the same vicious impulses as the speaker. 'Oh, baby, that god you been prayin' to / Is gonna give ya back what you're wishin' on someone else.' In their double role the figurings of 'New Pony' define a world enmeshed in depravity. This dual aspect of a violence which corrupts all better nature and which is both meted out and received by the speaker is maintained throughout the lyric. In the second stanza:

> Sometimes I wonder what's going on in the mind of Miss X
> You know she got such a sweet disposition
> I never know what the poor girl's gonna do to me next

What is worst is that the voice of the lyric finds itself addicted to the darkness of which it speaks. The failure of one pernicious mount, recorded in the first stanza, was borne only with pain:

> I had a pony, her name was Lucifer
> She broke her leg and needed shooting
> I swear it hurt me more than it could ever have hurted her

That Enemy Within

The bridling to a new darkness is reconfirmed in the closing stanza:

> Come over here pony, I, I wanna climb up one time on you
> Well, you're so bad and nasty
> But I love you, yes I do

The collision of opposing tendencies – the recognition of badness and the love of it – is caught in the second line here by the simultaneously standard American English sense of the words 'bad' and 'nasty' and that Black American English sense which has these words signify 'good', 'stylish', or 'admirable'.[9] In the face of a love of the standardly bad, that part of the speaker which is appalled by the 'shadow in the door' is paralysed. And it is in the face of such incapacitating love that the antiphonal voice of the chorus in the performance of 'New Pony' on *Street Legal* insistently and anxiously asks – 'How much longer?'

It is a question variously put in the lyrics from *Street Legal*. 'I fought with my twin, that enemy within, 'till both of us fell by the way' declares the speaker of 'Where Are You Tonight? (Journey Through Dark Heat)'. The last stanza of 'Señor' registers the suspense of waiting for renewed battle with the enemy. It also looks forward, in its allusion to Christ's cleansing of the Temple by overthrowing the tables of the moneychangers,[10] to Dylan's Christian lyrics and their drawing of the line of battle between graceful and malign powers in mind and world in terms of the Christian metaphysic of good and evil:

> Señor, senõr, let's disconnect these cables,
> Overturn these tables.
> This place don't make sense to me no more.
> Can you tell me what we're waiting for, señor?

6

To Separate the Good from the Bad

> Peace will come
> With tranquillity and splendor on the wheels of fire
> But will bring us no reward when her false idols fall
> And cruel death surrenders with its pale ghost retreating
> Between the King and the Queen of Swords
> 'Changing of the Guards', *Street Legal*

The temper of Dylan's overtly Christian lyrics – from the 1979 *Slow Train Coming* to the 1981 *Shot of Love* – is rarely that of withdrawal and quietude. Neither do the lyrics espouse the anti-mystical tendencies of a practical faith and piety. The dramatization of inner conflict so prevalent in Dylan's Christian verse has more a 'wire-drawn and tormented' spirit.[1]

The world of Dylan's Christian feeling is still the world he described in his 1962 'Song' to Woody Guthrie (*Bob Dylan*): 'sick ... hungry ... tired ... torn'. But one of the sharpest realizations of the Christian lyrics is of a world whose hunger and sickness lie beyond the capacity of human endeavour to satisfy and redeem. There is 'Trouble in the water, trouble in the air' in the second stanza of 'Trouble' from *Shot of Love*. And when, in the fifth stanza, some order is affirmed in the rhyme between 'legislature' and 'perverted nature' it is a consonance emphasizing only the deeper disorder that vitiates the enactment of all human laws:

> Nightclubs of the broken-hearted, stadiums of the damned,
> Legislature, perverted nature, doors that are rudely slammed.

Dylan's Christian verse frequently turns the unbelieving world's ridicule of faith against itself by casting the denial of spiritual reality as wishful thinking. In 'Property of Jesus' (*SOL*), the believer is called 'a loser 'cause he got no common sense / ... / 'Cause he doesn't tell you jokes or fairy tales ...' In 'Trouble', a secular self-reliance has the quality of desperate superstition, impotent against the disturbance of evil:

> You got your rabbit's foot, you got your good-luck charm.
> But they can't help you none when there's trouble.

Christianity grants a renewed impetus, within an explicitly transcendental frame of reference, to that Hebraic prophetic manner of berating the sins of the state which had characterized Dylan's earlier political lyrics. In 'When You Gonna Wake Up?' (*STC*), the varieties of degeneracy are listed with an economy appropriate to matters which are well known but which remain – for all that they are commonplaces, indeed *because* they are commonplaces – matters of life and death:

> You got innocent men in jail, your insane asylums are filled,
> You got unrighteous doctors dealing drugs that'll never cure your ills.

To Separate the Good from the Bad

> You got men who can't hold their peace and women who
>   can't control their tongues,
> The rich seduce the poor and the old are seduced by the
>   young.
>
> Adulterers in churches and pornography in the schools,
> You got gangsters in power and lawbreakers making rules.
>
> Spiritual advisors and gurus to guide your every move,
> Instant inner peace and every step you take has got to
>   be approved.

Spiritual advice is not exempt from the charge of spiritual vice. Nor is there exemption of any kind – however close to home – from the charge of spiritual consequence. 'You might be a rock 'n' role addict prancing on the stage, / You might have drugs at your command, women in a cage . . . // But you're gonna have to serve somebody': either 'the devil or . . . the Lord' ('Gotta Serve Somebody', *STC*). Dylan's Christian verse repeatedly stresses that there are no human choices that do not have absolute implications: 'Now there's spiritual warfare and flesh and blood breaking down. / Ya either got faith or ya got unbelief and there ain't no neutral ground' ('Precious Angel', *STC*). And more often than not it is the absolutely dire implications that are dwelt upon. The God of the Old Testament retains a large share in the Christian dispensation of these lyrics. 'God don't make promises that He don't keep' is the opening line of 'When You Gonna Wake Up?'. It may be that as the catalogue of the world's crimes increases throughout the lyric it is a promise of forgiveness to which we should be alert. But the line – like the tautness of the voice that sings it and the relentless pizzicato of the accompanying guitar notes in the performance on *Slow Train Coming* – is more aware of an inescapable threat. Its nervous wit is founded in dread and its certainty upon the invocation of a retributive God. In 'Gonna

To Separate the Good from the Bad

Change My Way of Thinking' (*STC*) we are reminded that 'There's a kingdom called Heaven, / A place where there is no pain of birth', but in this lyric even the Son shows less the merciful beauty of His countenance than the irresistible force of an uncompromising power:

> Jesus said, 'Be ready,
> For you know not the hour in which I come'.
> He said, 'He who is not for Me is against Me',
> Just so you know where He's coming from.

It is the urgency of Judgement which drives the slow train – where slow also means inexorably fast – in 'Slow Train'. In the performance on *Slow Train Coming* the voice that sings the words is driven by anxiety and it is anxiety that is echoed in the bending of the lead guitar notes that that voice plays with and against:

> You can't rely no more to be standin' around waitin'
> In the home of the brave, Jefferson turnin' over in his
>   grave,
> Fools glorifying themselves, trying to manipulate Satan
> And there's a slow, slow train comin' up around the bend.
>
> Big-time negotiators, false healers and woman haters,
> Masters of the bluff and masters of the proposition
> But the enemy I see wears a cloak of decency,
> All non-believers and men stealers talkin' in the name of
>   religion
> And there's a slow, slow train comin' up around the bend.

Measurement of the Last Things in Dylan's Christian lyrics is, in the last resort, ruled by a sense of the impending end of individual life. And the time that is so short is above all short for the master of bluff and proposition within the lyric-speaker's own identity. Time and again it is a conviction of his own depravity which traumatizes the speaker of these lyrics. 'Satan got you by the heel', the speaker of 'Dead Man, Dead Man' (*SOL*) warns that part of himself which is rooted in unredeemed nature, 'there's a bird's nest in your hair':

> Dead man, dead man,
> When will you arise?
> Cobwebs in your mind,
> Dust upon your eyes.

In the lyric 'Shot of Love' (*SOL*), a recoil from things of the world is a symptom of recoil from the sense of a mortal inadequacy in the soul: 'Don't show me no picture show or give me no book to read, / It don't satisfy the hurt inside nor the habit that it feeds'; where the unleavened circuit of a habit is maintained by a feeding that is at once a famishing. In 'Every Grain of Sand' (*SOL*) the self is its own tempter and it is not so much that the self tempts itself to evil as that the evil already resides *in* the temptation: 'I gaze into the doorway of temptation's angry flame / And every time I pass that way I always hear my name.' Nor, in the opening lines of this lyric, is the darkest voice of the personality quieted even at the moment when the self confesses, bewails and repents its own impurity. It is a recognition of the self's inherent capacity for evil that galvanizes even the most meditative of moods:

> In the time of my confession, in the hour of my deepest
>   need
> When the pool of tears beneath my feet flood every
>   newborn seed
> There's a dyin' voice within me reaching out somewhere,
> Toiling in the danger and in the morals of despair.

Don't have the inclination to look back on any mistake,
Like Cain, I now behold this chain of events that I must
   break.

A breaking with the demonic potencies of the soul is what so many of Dylan's Christian lyrics strive towards and what they find themselves unable unambiguously to affirm. The extremes between which these lyrics oscillate are, on the one hand, an assertion of the possibility of regeneration and, on the other, a sense of irreducible corruption in the soul, a certainty of alienation from grace that is indeed at times close to despair. In 'Dead Man, Dead Man' the dialogue with the darkest potentiality of the personality, the malign shadow of the psyche, raises more questions than the lyric can directly answer. In the second and last verses:

> Do you have any faith at all? Do you have any love to
>   share?
> The way that you hold your head, cursin' God with every
>   move . . .
>
> What are you tryin' to overpower me with, the doctrine or
>   the gun?
> My back is already to the wall, where can I run?
> The tuxedo that you're wearin', the flower in your lapel,
> Ooh, I can't stand it, I can't stand it,
> You wanna take me down to hell.

Unable to stand it, the self that would run from itself has nowhere to run except the apparent openness of the question in the last refrain: 'Dead man, dead man, / When will you arise?' But with the shadow never exorcized in the lyric the openness of the question is darkly weighted in favour of the darkest answer. Questions that fail to find exactly corresponding answers disturb

To Separate the Good from the Bad

the resolutions of a lyric such as 'When He Returns' (*STC*) no less forcefully:

> How long can I listen to the lies of prejudice?
> How long can I stay drunk on fear out in the wilderness?
> Can I cast it aside, all this loyalty and this pride?
>   .   .   .   .   .
> Surrender your crown on this blood-stained ground, take off your mask,
> He sees your deeds, He knows your needs even before you ask.
> How long can you falsify and deny what is real?
> How long can you hate yourself for the weakness you conceal?
> Of every earthly plan that be known to man, He is unconcerned...

But the verse remains fearfully concerned with the questions it accumulates and which its statements of faith never completely neutralize.

In 'Shot of Love' it is once more a question that emphasizes the pressure of unassimilated drives within the personality. The speaker in the fourth verse of this lyric imagines a considerable evil in order better to comprehend the nature of perfect Christian love – a love which, following the self-sacrificing example of Christ himself, should rise above even the greatest evil. Breaking the chain of events imagined here would be to break the vicious circle where violence is countered by an impulse that shares in the same taint of nature as the violence it is answering:

> Why would I want to take your life?
> You've only murdered my father, raped his wife,
> Tatooed my babies with a poison pen,
> Mocked my God, humiliated my friends.

To Separate the Good from the Bad

From the point of view of the natural man a love that would turn the other cheek to all this could be seen to constitute a mockery of the ordinary human affections. And while, from one perspective, the passage is formulated by the self that is committed to grasping just what Christ requires, there is at the same time a natural rebellion against the demands of that self taking place in the lines. A rebellion that turns on the word 'only'. 'You've *only* murdered my father, raped his wife. . . .' In its sarcasm this 'only' passes out of the control of the self that would sympathetically comprehend Christian love. In the bitter twist of that 'only' it is the natural self that breaks through – mocking Christian love by emphasizing how it may be seen to involve a debasement of human feeling and value. As it tries to imagine Christian love by imagining its opposite the verse itself confides a hopeless entanglement in the very realm it is trying to imagine beyond. Profoundly grasping the difficulty of the Christian conception of love and refusing glibly to claim possession of such love, the lyric bears witness to a sense of the impossibility of attaining it. Not surprising that the most the refrain of the lyric can rise to is the blank repetition: 'I need a shot of love, I need a shot of love.'

The desperation of fallen human nature is conceived from another angle in 'Heart of Mine' (*SOL*). In this lyric, one voice of self addresses another part of self over a matter of the heart. In the opening verse:

> Heart of mine be still,
> You can play with fire but you'll get the bill.
> Don't let her know
> Don't let her know that you love her.
> Don't be a fool, don't be blind
> Heart of mine.

To Separate the Good from the Bad

This voice can be heard, here and in the succeeding three verses, as that of a bland and narrow phase of mind, unattractive in its prudent assessment of the risks of feeling. The sterile accents of unadventurousness may be heard in the second stanza: 'Heart of mine go back home, / You got no reason to wander, you got no reason to roam. / . . . / Don't put yourself over the line / Heart of mine.' In the third verse the voice may be cowardly in its caution, mean in the prohibition it places upon desire and admiration:

> Heart of mine go back where you been,
> It'll only be trouble for you if you let her in.
> Don't let her hear
> Don't let her hear you want her.
> Don't let her know she's so fine
> Heart of mine.

The fearfulness, almost the paranoia, can be heard as more distinctly unpleaant when, in the fourth verse, the voice would impute faithlessness to the object of love: 'Heart of mine you know that she'll never be true, / She'll only give to others the love that she's gotten from you.' Against the slandering conservatism of this voice the heart may seem the *un*faint heart, the positive, passionate impulse that must risk all if it is to stand any chance of gaining all. Discretion never won fulfilment.

But if our sympathies may be so weighted against the voice of control in the first four stanzas, something happens in the fifth and final verse to complicate the issue. In this verse the voice shifts the terms of its address. It stops seeking simply to restrain and starts levelling accusations directly at the heart:

> Heart of mine so malicious and so full of guile,
> Give you an inch and you'll take a mile.
> Don't let yourself fall

> Don't let yourself stumble.
> If you can't do the time, don't do the crime
> Heart of mine.

The problem with these accusations and imputations is that they are not so easy to dismiss as the prudent cautionings. They may yet be the false and desperate charges of a questionable voice. But another possible perspective on the heart is opened up by the apparent cogency of the attack. The heart as spontaneous adventurer may mask the heart as cynical exploiter. This other heart is that which may declare a love it will not be able to sustain. It is the heart that may solicit a love which it will not be able, in the end, to reciprocate: 'If you can't do the time, don't do the crime.' The voice's prudence, looked at again, may be a voice of conscience, the voice of a caring self that is alienated by the irresponsible heart's capacity for causing damage. The lyric itself does not decide upon one or other reading of either the voice or the heart, for its subject is the questionable status of all the voices that speak within the loving self. What is explored in the self-address of this lyric is a corruption in the fabric of identity, a corruption whose most pernicious influence is to deny the self any objective grounds in its examination of its own nature and motivation in matters of the heart.

But if, in Dylan's Christian verse, a conviction of depravity traumatizes the lyric-speaker then it is at once a conviction that energizes speaker and lyrics. Imagining evil and spiritual death is the very life of these works. 'Love that's pure', insists the speaker of 'Watered-Down Love' (*SOL*), 'Won't sneak up into your room, tall, dark and handsome.' But it is the satanic insinuation that fires the imagination here as pure love is apprehended not in terms of itself but in terms of its antithesis. Comparably, in 'Dead Man, Dead Man', 'The tuxedo that you're wearin', the flower in your lapel, / Ooh, I can't stand it. . . .' Yet the perturbation is that

To Separate the Good from the Bad

that 'Ooh' sounds not simply resistance but a susceptibility to the seductive power of the shadowy self.

'Trouble in Mind' (1979)[2] is well aware of unmanageable compulsions:

> I got to know, Lord, when to pull back on the reins,
> Death can be the result of the most underrated pain.
> Satan whispers to ya, 'Well, I don't want to bore ya,
> But when ya get tired of the Miss So-and-so I got another
>   woman for ya'.

These are lines aware of the power of temptation and also acutely susceptible to temptations within such awareness. '"I don't want to bore ya, / But ..."'. The lines do not just acknowledge temptation, but collude with its knowing smile. When the speaker ends the lyric asking 'Lord, keep my blind side covered and see that I don't bleed', it is not merely protection from the temptation to exploit sexually that is needed, but protection from the capacity to exploit a humour in the recounting of such temptation. The vitality of this lyric again depends upon its realization of the defects it would seek to transcend. Entanglement with the conditions of spiritual death is the condition of its being: 'See that I don't bleed.' But the lyric is born of a spiritual bleeding: 'Trouble in mind, Lord, trouble in mind, / Lord, take away this trouble in mind.' For the trouble to be taken away would be to make the lyric unimaginable.

Similarly, a potent question is asked by the speaker in the third stanza of 'Precious Angel':

> My so-called friends have fallen under a spell.
> They look me squarely in the eye and they say, 'All is well'.
> Can they imagine the darkness that will fall from on high

To Separate the Good from the Bad

When men will beg God to kill them and they won't be
able to die?

The speaker may be haunted by the thought that his friends suffer a spiritual blindness born of an imaginative deficiency. But the lyric faces a spectre of another kind exactly because it *can* imagine darkness; the spectre that in entering imaginatively into darkness it necessarily partakes in the substance of that darkness. And the blackest feature of the imagining here is that it attributes to the highest light a power of the abysmal dark.

The loved one of 'Precious Angel', the 'Precious angel' herself, bears simultaneously literal and symbolic dimensions. 'Queen of my flesh' and 'lamp of my soul' to the speaker of the lyric, she is both human lover and anima-figure. At points she is apprehended by the speaker unreservedly as a messenger of grace, an ethereal/earthly emissary of the spirit of Christ the Son:

Precious angel, under the sun,
How was I to know you'd be the one
To show me I was blinded . . .

Shine your light, shine your light on me
Ya know I just couldn't make it by myself.
I'm a little too blind to see.

But there is a shadow to the positive aura of this figure. The disturbing possibilities that surface in the penultimate stanza ('We are covered in blood, girl, you know our forefathers were slaves') emerge fully in the final stanza, where recidivism threatens even the newest flight from bondage:

You're the queen of my flesh, girl, you're my woman,
   you're my delight,

You're the lamp of my soul, girl, and you torch up the
    night.
But there's violence in the eyes, girl, so let us not be
    enticed,
On the way out of Egypt, through Ethiopia, to the
    judgement hall of Christ.

The unqualified virtue of the 'Precious angel', as an enabler of imaginative vision and spiritual sight, is severely compromised in this passage. Imputed in a violent imbroglio of the profane and the sacred in the first two lines, she is complicit in the unregenerate and potentially unmanageable energies that are acknowledged in the third.

Comparably, the imaginative life of a lyric such as 'Gonna Change My Way of Thinking' (*STC*) is bred in confusion between dark and light energies. From the second to the third verses of this lyric an intuition of the force and extent of evil gives way to an image of redemptive power that, in its sado-masochistic ambience, appears gratuitously intimate with the sickness it is supposed to bear witness against. For all that Christ may be supposed to have taken on the sins of the world it is not clear that the effort of the human imagination to grasp a purifying energy can ever escape the disease it may yet imagine escaping:

So much oppression,
Can't keep track of it no more.
Sons becoming husbands to their mothers,
And old men turning young daughters into whores.

Stripes on your shoulders,
Stripes on your back and on your hands . . .
Swords piercing your side,
Blood and water flowing through the land.

To Separate the Good from the Bad

The speaker of 'Dead Man, Dead Man' admits intense frustration at his own sickness of soul:

> Uttering idle words from a reprobate mind,
> Clinging to strange promises, dying on the vine,
> Never bein' able to separate the good from the bad . . .

But Dylan's Christian lyrics recurrently disclose the sense in which a realm of the absolutely pure and good stands in contradiction to the creative premise of the utterances that posit that realm. It is necessarily the 'dyin' voice' that speaks in Dylan's Christian lyrics and it is the inalienably fallen status of the imagination itself which those lyrics finally confirm. Nor is there a safe and saving limit incorporated into that confirmation. The overwhelming question put by Dylan's Christian lyrics is whether the life of the imagination does not have its very roots in a chaos where powers of terror and destruction and powers of a healing grace are inextricably confused. The Christian lyrics reach both backwards and forwards in Dylan's writing to those of his works which, contemplating the ultimate ground of the human soul and imagination, emphasize neither the good nor the bad, neither the dark nor the light, neither horror nor grace, but a point of infinite regression where such distinctions collapse and disappear.

7
That Forbidden Zone

... the dazzling obscurity of the secret Silence, outshining all brilliance with the intensity of ... Darkness. ... He is neither ... greatness, nor smallness; nor equality, nor inequality; nor similarity, nor dissimilarity ... neither does He live, nor is He life ... neither can the reason attain to him ... neither is He ... the false, nor the true; nor can any affirmation or negation be applied to Him. ...
                        Dionysius the Areopagite, *The Mystical Theology*

... God must be very I, I very god ... this he and this I, to wit, God and the soul. ... a not-God, a not-spirit, a not-Person, a not-image ... alien from all duality.
                                  Meister Eckhart, *Sermon XCIX*

The simultaneously thrilling and forbidding complexion of spaces beyond the limits of the social and the rational, and the confusion of gratulation and desperation involved in transgressing those limits, were hinted at by André Breton when he spoke of the unconscious as 'the forbidden zone'.[1] A comparable hint informs Dylan's use of the same phrasing in a version of the last stanza of 'Tangled Up in Blue' which he performed at Brussels on 7 June 1984. As we saw in chapter 4, the version of this stanza performed in London on 7 July 1984 preluded a statement of yearning for an archetypal Other ('We always did love the very

That Forbidden Zone

same one / We just saw her from a different point of view') with the words: 'So now I'm goin' on back again / Maybe tomorrow or maybe next year.' But the Brussels version had framed the account of desire for a condition beyond the pale of self and narrative by beginning: 'So now I'm goin' on back again / To that forbidden zone.'[2] The disconcertions touched on in the Brussels formulation are the overriding concern of many Dylan lyrics. And, not least, of the 1966 *Blonde on Blonde* lyric, 'Visions of Johanna'.

'I watch upon your scorpion / Who crawls across your circus floor', cries the speaker of 'Temporary Like Achilles' to his lover, in lines that touch the combination of menace and disorientation that is characteristic of most of the lyrics from (or associated with) *Blonde on Blonde*.[3] The atmosphere of the *Blonde on Blonde* lyrics is one in which the uncertain may masquerade as the reassuringly obvious: 'Fifteen jugglers' and 'Five believers / All dressed like men', announces the speaker of 'Obviously Five Believers', 'Tell yo' mama not to worry because / They're just my friends.' But neither friendship nor love can be taken for granted in the *Blonde on Blonde* lyrics. The world of those lyrics is one of doubtful insinuation: 'Now you stand here while your finger's goin' up my sleeve' ('She's Your Lover Now'). It is a world redolent with possibilities of failed insight and veiled motivation: 'I couldn't see what you could show me / Your scarf had kept your mouth well hid' ('One of Us Must Know (Sooner or Later)').

Like certain other lyrics of *Blonde on Blonde*, 'Stuck Inside of Mobile with the Memphis Blues Again' is steeped in a sense of physical invasion that at once defines psychological encroachment:

> Mona tried to tell me
> To stay away from the train line,
> She said that all the railroad men

> Just drink up your blood like wine.
> An' I said, 'Oh, I didn't know that,
> But then again, there's only one I met
> An' he just smoked my eyelids
> An' punched my cigarette'.

Steeped in and drained by. Frustration and impotence are captured in the image at the opening of 'Stuck Inside of Mobile' of a figure unable to generate anything except a series of noughts:

> Oh, the ragman draws circles
> Up and down the block.
> I'd ask him what the matter was
> But I know that he don't talk.

A world of shifting grounds and unstable forces, this is a world that can shroud its gravest proclivities within a perverse humour, as in 'I Wanna Be Your Lover':

> Well, the undertaker in his midnight suit
> Says to the masked man, 'Ain't you cute!'
> Well the mask man he gets up on the shelf
> And he says, 'You ain't so bad yourself'.

But it is in 'Visions of Johanna' that the cardinal tendencies of the *Blonde on Blonde* group of lyrics appear in their deepest vein. 'Visions of Johanna' violates the logic of consecutive statement more cruelly than perhaps any other Dylan lyric. A summary of the work might say that it presents a consciousness engaged – during what is, at least in the early stages of the lyric, a night-time vigil – in reflecting upon various matters that concern it. Perspective and objects of attention slide and transform themselves throughout. But there is a constant in that the consciousness returns at the end of each of the five stanzas to its experience of certain visions which threaten to overwhelm – and, indeed, by the conclusion of the lyric *do* overwhelm – all other considerations.

The first line of 'Visions of Johanna' warns us that the lyric's terms of reference are the unreliability of terms of reference. In this opening line even the notation of a principle of uncertainty is framed not as a statement but as a question, as if a certain uncertainty might be too sure of itself: 'Ain't it just like the night to play tricks when you're tryin' to be so quiet?' Implications of trickery and mischief, involutions of illusion and deception, are endemic to 'Visions of Johanna'. The order of confusion in the lyric is such that in the opening four lines of the second stanza the 'night watchman' is unable to measure himself in relation to incoherence. The line between reason and unreason upon which the constructions of logic depend is blurred for the night watchman just as it is blurred in the surrealistic register of the lyric's language. The sense of a suspension of rational measure and control is emphasized even by the image of the night watchman clicking his flashlight. The detail of the flashlight invokes the metaphor of a light shining in darkness and raises the possibility of explanation and clarification. But the stock metaphor is called up only as a ghost of itself. It is raised only to be parodied. For the image of a light flashing works here not to celebrate enlightenment but to confirm a greater darkness, a larger unintelligibility. All's *not* well with a world where the watcher upon the night, the guardian of the day's order through the hours of darkness, has lost his bearings:

> In the empty lot where the ladies play blindman's bluff
>   with the key chain
> And the all-night girls they whisper of escapades out on
>   the 'D' train

> We can hear the night watchman click his flashlight
> Ask himself if it's him or them that's really insane

In the first two lines of this passage the forces that deprive sanity of its ground are characterized by elements that recall and amplify those introduced in the opening line of the lyric. Words and phrases in these two lines provoke associations not only with the darkness of night-time but also with the darkness of blindness. And the night whose trickery had in the first line of the lyric thwarted any attempt at silence here finds – through the 'all-night girls' – a voice. Only it is the unsettling voice of undertone and innuendo, hardly speech at all, the near-inarticulation that gestures towards secrets it does not disclose. Dissociation from a predictable pattern of events, together with a labyrinthine obscurity, are suggested in the whisperings of mysterious happenings on a line of the New York subway. It is an effect of dissociation intensified by the juxtaposition of the romantically unspecific – whispered 'escapades' – with the literally, perhaps basely, specific – 'the "D" train'. The 'escapades' hinted at by the girls echo the game-playing of the 'ladies' in the preceding line which in turn hearks back to the night's 'play' of 'tricks' at the start of the lyric. Nor is the ladies' game more legitimate than the subversive 'tricks' of the night. It is an instance of the cheating word-play of 'Visions of Johanna' that the ladies do not play 'blindman's buff', but 'blindman's bluff'.

Play appears in 'Visions of Johanna' not as an allowed and tame diversion from the order of the adult world but as a type of the powers that that order seeks to contain and discipline. Like the ecstatic freedom of childhood imagination, which may appear alien, inimical, threatening to the consciousness of adults, play enters 'Visions of Johanna' as an anarchic potency. A force that in its unimpeded *jouissance* challenges the responsibilities of rational culture. A force that in all its manifestations of deceit, trickery and illusion undermines the security of licensed forms and structures. The condition of the night in 'Visions of Johanna' is instinct with these displacing, subterranean energies of the psyche. And it is these irrepressible energies that are the object of the visions that give the lyric its title. By the end of the first verse the trickster night of the initial line expands for the speaker of the lyric into 'these visions of Johanna that conquer my mind'.

The idea of a slipping of rules and confinement is present throughout 'Visions of Johanna'. It conditions the use of a single word such as 'escapades'. More complexly, the interactions of freedom and constraint inhabit the compound image of the 'key chain' in the first line of the second stanza. But it is the fourth stanza that offers one of the lyric's most relentless imaginings of the breakdown of recognized and sanctioned form. In the first line of this stanza, museum-keeping as an attempt to preserve artificially a stability of forms is mocked as an enterprise that vainly sets out to test and judge infinity by the productions of time. The second line takes such longevity as cultural products held in museums may acquire and suggests that the very ideal of immutability – at least so long as it is conceived as a kind of indefinite duration – is something burdensome. The third and fourth lines go further in suggesting the sense of entrapment that may be associated with any attempt to establish unchanging forms, rules and privileges, aesthetic or otherwise. Frustration with the fixities of a classical canon is pictured acutely and comically as being experienced from within the canon. Established orders are not modified simply from without, but themselves contain the seeds of their own exhaustion. The colloquialism which here defines the Mona Lisa's unease – her boredom with her own status – itself constitutes an affront to and an erosion of the laws of approved respect that conventionally hem her in. And if artistic respectability neutralizes the enigma of

That Forbidden Zone

the Mona Lisa's smile, a revisioning of that smile in these lines renders it once more mutable and unsafe:

> Inside the museums, Infinity goes up on trial
> Voices echo this is what salvation must be like after a while
> But Mona Lisa musta had the highway blues
> You can tell by the way she smiles

The succeeding four lines of this stanza envision a reduction of form to primal elements as – in an image that itself displaces Marcel Duchamp's rendering of the Mona Lisa in the painting *LHOOQ* (1919) – even gender difference becomes confused and human contour and feature are erased:

> See the primitive wallflower freeze
> When the jelly-faced women all sneeze
> Hear the one with the mustache say, 'Jeeze
> I can't find my knees'

As unaccommodated forces dissolve contour and feature, so too the certainties of nominal identity are usurped in 'Visions of Johanna'. Thus the speaker, at the end of the second stanza: '... these visions of Johanna have now taken my place.' The game of blindman's buff, in which 'one player is blindfolded and tries to catch and identify any one of the others, who, on their part, push him about' (*OED*), serves as a touchstone of the disorientation of consciousness that pervades 'Visions of Johanna'. Disturbance of the surface structure of the self is implied throughout the lyric in the elusiveness of the point of view from which it is spoken. Throughout, the speaker's self is splintered and reconstituted in a multi-faceted assemblage of personal pronouns and names. An apt analogy for the effect would be the perspectival incongruity of a cubist painting. Thus the 'fiddler' and the 'peddler' in the

That Forbidden Zone

final stanza, or, in the third stanza, 'little boy lost' who 'takes himself so seriously', may all read as potencies of the speaker's own personality. Again, in the room described in the first stanza there are apparently just two literal individuals, the speaker and his lover. But settling on a number does not contain the situation. For even if at a literal level there are only two people, at another level the speaker is refracted into several through his self-objectification in second- and third-person pronouns and through his voyeuristic observation of himself as that person who is the lover of 'Louise'. The self-distancing that takes place in this stanza enforces a distinction – among others – between the self that performs the role of lover and the self that is aware of visions that are taking over the mind. In this, as in the following stanzas of the lyric, plural perspectives and multiple selves find a point of focus only in visions of something that is Other than those perspectives and those selves:

> Ain't it just like the night to play tricks when you're tryin' to be so quiet?
> We sit here stranded, though we're all doin' our best to deny it
> And Louise holds a handful of rain, temptin' you to defy it
> Lights flicker from the opposite loft
> In this room the heat pipes just cough
> The country music station plays soft
> But there's nothing, really nothing to turn off
> Just Louise and her lover so entwined
> And these visions of Johanna that conquer my mind

As the visions threaten to overwhelm the reflecting consciousness of the speaker of the lyric so they remain uncontained by any simple narrative structure. In the first stanza, visions in the middle of the night are set as the speaker's present experience:

'these visions... that conquer'. The second stanza can be taken as reiterating, albeit with a slight shift in perspective, the nocturnal standpoint taken up in the first. In the fifth line of this verse, 'Louise, she's all right, she's just near' while in the concluding line: 'these visions... have now taken my place.' But at the end of the third stanza the visions are offered as happening at a time that lies beyond the passing of the night: 'And these visions of Johanna, they kept me up past the dawn.' In the first two stanzas of 'Visions of Johanna' there is no radical disjunction between the speaker's situation in the present and the experience of the visions. What the end of the third stanza momentarily allows us to glimpse is a split between the visionary experience and that part of the speaker's identity that is bound up in history and time. In the curious formulation of the last line here the speaker speaks from a present perspective that recognizes its position at a later point in time than the situation of the night: 'they kept me up past the dawn.' There is registered simultaneously, however, another 'present' – the continuing experience of 'these' visions. The undifferentiated present of the continuing visions forms a matrix which underlies and undermines any straightforward narrative or sequential continuity in the work. In the fourth stanza the present of the visions is unplaced in relation either to the night-time or to the post-dawn. Inside the museums infinity goes up on trial and in the last line 'these visions of Johanna, they make it all seem so cruel.' When, at the end of the final stanza, 'these visions of Johanna are now all that remain', it is chronology they have removed as well as everything else. 'Deep in our soul we have no past.'[4] In 'Visions of Johanna' the medium of the visionary present – a present that slips formal synchrony with the past – is used to gesture towards a power that exceeds temporal stricture, that exceeds division between night and day, just as it exceeds the speaker's familiar selves.

Exceeding the familiar, it is a power that exceeds not least human love. In the second stanza the nature of the self-definition – the self-imaging or self-reflection – that is achieved through loving another human being is brought under severe scrutiny. As the night watchman questions his own sanity the speaker returns to the thought of Louise. 'Louise, she's all right, she's just near / She's delicate.' But she only '*seems* like the mirror'. The status and value of that definition of himself which the speaker finds through his relationship with Louise is called in doubt. Louise as lover, providing only an apparent self-definition, is utterly surpassed by the stirrings of the psyche designated in the visions of Johanna. The sheer measurability of Louise as human lover emphasizes the extent to which the relationship of lovers does not tap resources comparable to the energy now pressing upon the speaker's mind. Not that the visionary present is confused with presence. In the final two lines of the stanza it is still only visions or intimations of daemonic energy that destroy the living reality of Louise and usurp the ordinary self of the speaker:

> Louise, she's all right, she's just near
> She's delicate and seems like the mirror
> But she just makes it all too concise and too clear
> That Johanna's not here
> The ghost of 'lectricity howls in the bones of her face
> Where these visions of Johanna have now taken my place

It is against the background of the uncompromising authority of the visions that the dramas of the ordinary self are unflatteringly reviewed in stanza three. That self's preoccupation with images of its own significance and suffering, its preoccupation with sentiment and its elegaic commitment to time, appear here a matter of naïve posturing, a conviction of identity misconceived, misplaced and impotent:

> Now, little boy lost, he takes himself so seriously
> He brags of his misery, he likes to live dangerously
> And when bringing her name up
> He speaks of a farewell kiss to me
> He's sure got a lotta gall to be so useless and all
> Muttering small talk at the wall while I'm in the hall

The 'blatancy', as John Herdman has put it,[5] of those concentrated end and internal rhymes ('gall/all/small/wall/hall') captures at once the little boy's embarrassing self-parade and the speaker's disdain for that parade of self. But little boy and speaker, if not one person, are not separate people. And, as the next lines reveal, a sense of uselessness depletes even the self that scorns the impotence of the self. In the end there appears to be strength only in the visions:

> How can I explain?
> Oh, its so hard to get on
> And these visions of Johanna, they kept me up past
>   the dawn

The politics of the decentred self and its relationships are further explored in the fifth stanza, whose opening five lines bespeak a world in which pretence interacts with pretence, a world of masquerade where a trifler is the victim of a sham and where even cynicism is cynically mannered:

> The peddler now speaks to the countess who's pretending
>   to care for him
> Sayin', 'Name me someone that's not a parasite and I'll go
>   out and say a prayer for him'
> But like Louise always says

'Ya can't look at much, can ya man?'
As she, herself, prepares for him

The tangled transactions of an unregenerate world together with the ennui that informs those transactions are formally dispensed with in the concluding stanza. Where stanzas one and three had nine lines and two and four ten lines, the fifth stanza has fourteen. The expansion allows for a pattern of seven rhyming lines beginning with line six. The rhymes of these seven lines, starting with 'showed' and climaxing with 'explodes', enact the sense of a violent disposal of constraint, the removal of a repression. After the explosion all that remains are the visions of Johanna. The worldly encumbrances and appearances that the energy of those visions sweeps away includes certain stereotypes of women. If woman as lover has been stripped of life by the visions, and if woman as 'master' piece has been unfixed, the fifth stanza has the power of those visions exposing not only the countess, not only woman as rich dissembler, but also woman as sanctified mother. Invoked, that figure simply fails to appear as mediator or sustainer of the self that is under stress. And in the seventh and eighth lines the entrapments of the stereotypical role dissolve as Madonna's 'cage', where 'her cape of the stage once had flowed', disintegrates and space is utterly cleared for the visions of Johanna. Whatever may be thought of Johanna, hers is again the 'feminine' that is not to be caught within positions prescribed for the female. Eluding such positions, eluding rational and narrative ordering, eluding the nexus of debt and ethical responsibility that the world seeks to operate, Johanna also eludes fixture within the words of this lyric. However much the visions threaten to ruin time, the lyric remains a feature of those ruins. The point in the verse at which it is said that nothing remains of worldly things, or where all that remains are remains, the point where the ordinary self has been overwhelmed, is the point at which the lyric stops.

For it cannot speak the unspeakable. Throughout, the lyric does not and cannot say directly what Johanna is, it only says and can only say what she is not. To the extent that she remains, she remains, in Mallarmé's words, that 'air or song beneath the text'.[6] An air that the text here hints at through images of play which confess their unearthly musical implication only in the penultimate line of the work: 'The harmonicas play the skeleton keys....'. Gesturing indirectly towards Johanna, 'Visions of Johanna' gestures towards something outside itself. Doing that it evokes doors opening on spaces where the boundary between life and death is erased. 'Skeleton keys and the rain':

> Madonna, she still has not showed
> We see this empty cage now corrode
> Where her cape of the stage once had flowed
> The fiddler, he now steps to the road
> He writes ev'rything's been returned which was owed
> On the back of the fish truck that loads
> While my conscience explodes
> The harmonicas play the skeleton keys and the rain
> And these visions of Johanna are now all that remain

Magical and perilous. Visionary and deathly. There is ambivalence in 'Visions of Johanna' concerning the unquestioned power of the visions. From one point of view the 'rain' is a visionary rain, signalling access to an area of fertile resource. But 'Louise holds a handful of rain, temptin' you to defy it.' For all that the visions expose the vanity of human practices, for all that they offer release from the confinement of worldly forms, the consciousness of the lyric is wracked, tempted to resist the visions it is compelled by. The visions find their power, after all, not in human sympathy but in despite of it. Louise might well tempt towards defiance. For she and the common human affections are obliterated by the visions. And the earthly self does not lightly forfeit those affections. When the speaker speaks of visions that 'conquer my mind', he at once speaks in sympathy with the conqueror and feels the burden of the conquered. 'Visions of Johanna', witnessing to a more than mortal sight, is full of suggestions less of an earthly fertility than of a visionary emptiness: 'nothing, really nothing', 'the empty lot', 'Voices echo', 'empty cage'. It hints at the reduction, under a greater force, of the known world's *élan vital*: 'Lights flicker', 'heat pipes just cough', 'music station plays soft', 'really nothing to turn off.' But the lyric has also edges of complaint against the intolerable demands of the visionary: 'We sit here stranded', 'to be so useless', 'it's so hard to get on', 'they kept me up.' There is terror, as well as delight, at the disappearance of form: '"Jeeze / I can't find my knees."' It is not just a criticism of Louise, but evidence of rising alarm at the corrosive power of the visions that Louise should make it 'all too ... clear' that she is not Johanna. Similarly, at the end of the fourth stanza, material riches and the promise of goals seen in the distance may drive the labours and relieve the burdens of the ordinary world, but it is painful that the visions should make all such things seem dumbly pedantic: 'Oh, jewels and binoculars hang from the head of the mule / But these visions of Johanna, they make it all seem so cruel.'

Something of the ambivalence of attitude in the lyric is measured in the technical features of the verse. The whispering assonances, the haunting incertitudes of the partial rhymes, the lassitude of the double and triple rhymes, the consonantal softness of the masculine rhymes, and the enervations of the inordinately extended lines, may on the one hand imply the entropy of a world succumbing to a power larger than itself. On the other hand, it may also convey the reluctance of that world and its consciousness to submit to annihilation. From this point of view it is not weakness we hear, reading the lines or listening to the extreme tardiness of the performance of the lyric on *Blonde on*

Blonde, but the weariness and exhaustion of intense resistance. From this point of view, when the visions are at last all that remain, it is not so much a moment of victory as of defeat: almost that the worst – delayed for as long as the lyric form could delay – has at last happened.

The power of the visions may be in some sense an affirmable power. But as a power preluded by an explosion of conscience it may be something more alien, something that refuses management in terms of either affirmation or disaffirmation. The rain at the end touches a deep foreboding. 'Visions of Johanna' raises a dread that the daemonic charge that 'howls in the bones' of Louise's face and plays the 'skeleton keys' may be not only humanly intolerable, but intolerant of the human. Visions of the anima, visions of the forbidden zone, may amount to visions of Gehenna, glimpses into a zone that for the mortal self spells only relentless pain. Such intolerance – the mystic inhumanity of a principle that surpasses the divisions and multiplicities of the formed world – Dylan was to revision in the 1983 *Infidels* lyric 'I and I'.

'I gave my heart to know wisdom . . .'; 'I looked on all the works that my hands had wrought . . . and, behold, all was vanity and vexation of spirit, and there was no profit under the sun' (Ecclesiastes 1:17; 2:11). 'I and I' invokes the inward gaze of the Book of Ecclesiastes as, in the third of its five stanzas, its speaker pictures a journey taken beyond the charted terms of the day-to-day self, beyond worldly values and preoccupations. Ecclesiastes 9:11, telling of the emptiness of earthly success, 'I . . . saw under the sun, that the race is not to the swift, nor the battle to the strong', is reworked in the first line of the verse:

> Took an untrodden path once, where the swift don't win the race,
> It goes to the worthy, who can divide the word of truth.

> Took a stranger to teach me, to look into justice's
>   beautiful face
> And to see an eye for an eye and a tooth for a tooth.

A tissue of allusions to both Old and New Testaments ('Study to shew thyself approved unto God . . . rightly dividing the word of truth', 2 Timothy 2:15; 'eye for eye, tooth for tooth: as he hath caused a blemish in a man, so shall it be done to him again', Leviticus 24:20) compounds the image of engagement with a principle transcending the contingent and the relative: a principle of total truth, total justice, total beauty.

The same absolutist note is struck once more in the four line refrain which separates each verse of 'I and I' and which concludes the lyric. The refrain may read as dramatizing a contrast between a self constituted in the imperfection of the formed world and another ground of identity that shares in the nature of ultimate reality. The phrase 'I and I' – glancing at the Rastafarian formulation which may signify 'myself and God' – prepares for the allusion in the fourth line to the word of God in Exodus 33:20: 'And he said, thou canst not see my face: for there shall no man see me, and live':

> I and I
> In creation where one's nature neither honors nor
>   forgives.
> I and I
> One says to the other, no man sees my face and lives.

The idea of a divine face within the psyche which exceeds the bounds of the quotidian self may be traced again in the movement of the lyric as a whole. 'I and I' opens:

> Been so long since a strange woman has slept in my bed.
> Look how sweet she sleeps, how free must be her dreams.

> In another lifetime she must have owned the world, or
>   been faithfully wed
> To some righteous king who wrote psalms beside moonlit
>   streams.

In the first line and a half here the state of sleep is apprehended, as it were, from the outside. But the high valuation placed on sleep turns into an interior validation of dream and then of imagination itself as the speaker moves from straightforward observation, first, to a projection of what the woman's dreams must be like and, secondly, to the generation of images whose ideality is felt to match that absorption in the unconscious which is the woman's estate. And while the woman's unselfconsciousness remains a term of value in itself, the subject of the lines is simultaneously that potency of the speaker's own subjectivity which generates ideal imaginings. The enviable otherness of the sleeping woman from her own waking self and from the observing speaker modulates into the otherness that is the speaker's own capacity for imaginative projection. The terms of the projection are frankly mythopoeic or fabulous. The stories can even vary ('owned the world, *or* been faithfully wed') but the anti-historical, pre-lapsarian figuring remains the same. They are figurings in which religious connotations fuse with implications of a state of ideal creativity. Yet there is no easy inhabiting of these figurings. The sense of wonder in the passage, its preoccupation with strangeness, defines not only the woman but the unfamiliarity to the speaker's own natural self of those imaginative projections by which he constructs other lifetimes and other worlds. And the wonder touches a melancholy that measures the distance between history and an ideal condition. It is a melancholy that by the same token measures a gap between the speaker's consciously observing self and that imaginative soul whose roots draw deeply on dream and the unconscious. Implied in the melancholy of the passage is the speaker's own self-alienation. It is a point made more explicit when, in the second verse of 'I and I', attention shifts from the other life of sleep and the imagination to the matter of *this* lifetime.

The shift is abrupt and shocking:

> Think I'll go out and go for a walk,
> Not much happenin' here, nothin' ever does.
> Besides, if she wakes up now, she'll just want me to talk
> I got nothin' to say, 'specially about whatever was.

Imaginative reverie is displaced and the speaker returns forlornly to the sole self of his ordinary consciousness and life. A sense of the tedium of that self and its experience directs the entire passage. Implied in the last two lines is the possibility of a long-standing relationship between the speaker and the woman: 'she'll just want me to talk / I got nothin' to say, 'specially about whatever was.' The woman's foreignness in the first stanza need not be that of a literal stranger, but may simply define the difference that is mysteriously enforced by sleep from the known and familiar person of everyday experience. Returning to her own waking self – and re-establishing the terms of what is, to the speaker at least, an *over*familiar and even exhausted reality – she would only exacerbate his frustration at the common run of things. It is once this point concerning a dissatisfaction with the known and the domestic has been established in the second verse that the lyric moves on, in the third stanza, to the speaker's recollection of once having been shown – appropriately by a stranger – beyond the scope of the everyday world. And it is towards untrodden paths that a part of the speaker remains oriented in the present of the lyric.

The force of that orientation is apparent again in the fourth stanza. Here the capacity for renewal within the created order of things is registered by the speaker on his walk with a profound sense of ennui. Rebirth within nature – renewal turning cyclically upon renewed death – is a doubtful principle of regeneration. The spiritual gaze of the speaker is such that even a thought of the end of the world itself inspires no unease. Imagination may claim to be unaffected by and apocalyptically unconcerned at the failure of the contingent:

> Outside of two men on a train platform there's nobody in sight,
> They're waiting for spring to come, smoking down the track.
> The world could come to an end tonight, but that's alright.
> She should still be there sleepin' when I get back.

The fifth and final stanza of 'I and I' witnesses an intensification of the metaphorical spiritual journey. Wilful excursion by night is accelerated in this verse into determined incursion by day. Paths inward that lie deeper than the speaking self seem governed now by a kind of necessity. However adept the worldly self may be in sustaining worldly realities – for its own sake or for the sake of others – it is an adeptness founded in a compulsion to push beyond the pale of the socialized self:

> Noontime, and I'm still pushin' myself along the road, the darkest part,
> Into the narrow lanes, I can't stumble or stay put.
> Someone else is speakin' with my mouth, but I'm listening only to my heart.
> I've made shoes for everyone, even you, while I still go barefoot.

A deepening of the journey and a special kind of darkening. The final verse of 'I and I' heightens complications that may be felt throughout the lyric concerning a model of identity that accords wholly positive value to the soul at the expense of disparaging the mundane aspects of personality. The 'I' that speaks in this verse seeks at one level to express the interest of that side of the psyche that can be neither directly seen nor, indeed, articulated. The '[s]omeone else' in the third line may be the self of common experience. The 'you' in the last line may be an unspecified other person, perhaps the woman mentioned at the outset of the lyric, or even a putative, exemplary member of the lyric's audience, but it also includes the signification of the speaker's own habitual self: addressed, as it were, from the point of view of the soul. The opening lines may read as the deeper self's insistence that it must not be deflected from its deepest direction: 'Noontime, and I'm still pushin' myself...' But, 'I *can't* ... stay put.' The voluntary sympathy with the face that cannot be seen mingles with the accent of necessity: the sense of not being able to do otherwise than drive deeper. If this 'I' claims a sympathy with the absolute it lays claim, after all, to an alignment with imperatives that – in the completeness of their authority – refuse any easy notion of difference or choice. This 'I' invokes an authority which threatens its own status as a separate agent. As an 'I' – a self-consciousness and a word – it does itself have a stake in the realm of division that is the world of ordinary human experience. The 'I' of the last stanza of 'I and I' may distinguish itself from '[s]omeone else' speaking, but in articulating the interest of the absolute it is caught in self-contradiction. The splittings of the 'I' in this lyric implicitly regress further than the nominal doubling of the title and refrain. Inherently divided against itself the speaking 'I' of the last stanza at once pushes and feels the weight of being pushed. It drives towards something that it is simultaneously unwilling to drive towards. And a part of what it fears in that unwillingness is that the object it partly wishes to affirm may not be unreservedly desirable.

To tread untrodden paths, in the concluding verse of 'I and I', is to undertake a journey fraught with possibilities of constriction and disorientation: 'pushin' ... / Into the narrow lanes'. It is, moreover, to pursue a path whose destination is ominously obscure: 'Noontime', the zenith of the day, but 'the *darkest* part'. These may be ultimate areas, but passing outside the known is not necessarily to enter a realm of unconditioned sweetness and light. There is an honest and fearful consistency in the brooding apprehension of absoluteness in 'I and I'. The lyric grasps profoundly that to approach the synthesis of the absolute may be to venture beyond the very structures that enable distinctions between contraries to be made. Admitting neither division nor condition the absolute may exclude or, equally, may include neither the light nor the dark, neither the positive nor the negative. And going barefoot may be to tread stripped of the protections against the undivided intensity of the divine that a familiar, imperfect world of contrasts and oppositions paradoxically allows. There is an inflexion of anxiety in the last stanza of 'I and I' that echoes the urgency of Isaiah 59: 10: 'we stumble at noonday as in the night; we are in desolate places as dead men.' Isaiah famously prefigures the possibility of redemption through the agency of a purely generous and forgiving God: 'the Lord's hand is not shortened, that it cannot save: neither his ear heavy, that it cannot hear' (59: 1). But no one-sided attribution concerning God reassures 'I and I'. The absolute here – whether of truth or of beauty – admits of no qualification. Its justice – disallowing those discriminations that, in the name of mercy, are sometimes allowed to compromise an absolute condition – works with savagely exact equations: 'a tooth for a tooth'. The last phrase of the refrain of 'I and I' registers the dread that may accompany recognition of the absolute as wholly Other. It registers the kind of 'numinous' moment whose 'awe-inspiring character', as Rudolf Otto has put it, is 'gravely disturbing to those ... who recognise nothing in the divine nature but goodness, gentleness, love, and a sort of confidential intimacy, in a word, only those aspects of God which turn towards the world of men'.[7] It registers, in short, without temporization or rationalization, the featureless countenance of the more-than-human: 'no man sees my face and lives.'

One of the most troubled moments of 'I and I' lies in the second line of the refrain. This might indeed signal the state of human nature within a corrupted world. But from another point of view it can hint at the way in which the divine pulse within personality that would exchange an 'eye for an eye' may severely and uncompromisingly enter mortal experience, so that 'one's nature neither honors nor forgives'. A dimension of the melancholy that complicates the mood of the first two stanzas of 'I and I', and an aspect of the desolation that is one of the tones of the final verse, define a regret that the compulsively valued energies of the soul should draw from so far beyond the limits of the human. There is a sadness in the observation of the woman sleeping which recognizes that no amount of ideal imaginings of her other lifetimes will really compensate for the soul's terrible dismissal of her in this lifetime. It is an anguish that the heart's inexorable wisdom should touch such denials of feeling. 'Sometimes', Dylan observed in 1985, 'the "you" in my songs is me talking to me.... The "I", like in "I and I", also changes. It could be I or it could be the "I" who created me.'[8] The changing tonal perspectives of 'I and I' move ambiguously around irreconcilable points of reference in identity. Wracked between human sympathy and a mystic apprehension of ultimate reality that involves a negation of distinction between the positive and the negative, the lyric roots itself in a contradictoriness from which it does not pretend to offer avenues of escape. No more does the other major lyric from *Infidels*, 'Jokerman', deal in clarification or rationalization. Like 'I and I', 'Jokerman' takes its stand on a field of irresolvable tension. But while 'I and I' and 'Jokerman' share certain ground in common, there is a difference in focus between the two lyrics. The tensions of 'Jokerman' are founded less in a vision of profound contradictoriness than in a vision of embracing indeterminacy.

'"There must be some way out of here", said the joker to the thief.' Thus the opening line of the 1968 lyric in four stanzas, 'All Along the Watchtower' (*JWH*). The joker is complaining at the way in which his own creative resources and productions – sacramental, fecund – are exploited and consumed by worldly powers: '"Businessmen, they drink my wine, plowmen dig my earth, / None of them along the line know what any of it is worth."' Joker and 'thief' speak in this lyric as aspects of a personality engaged in self-dialogue. And the voice of self as thief seeks to temper the joker's apparent indignation. After all, in the deals negotiated between imagination and the world, it may not be entirely straightforward who is stealing from whom. '"Let us not talk falsely now"', advises the thief at the end of the second stanza, '"the hour is getting late."' Nevertheless, the joker's dissatisfaction with things as they are and the thief's discriminating sense of urgency combine to inform – in the lyric's closing couplet verses – a warning of radical change at hand:

> All along the watchtower, princes kept the view
> While all the women came and went, barefoot servants, too.
>
> Outside in the distance a wildcat did growl,
> Two riders were approaching, the wind began to howl.

But a change for the better? What do these signs portend and whose interests do they serve? The menace in these last lines of 'All Along the Watchtower' might be directed simply against the enslavements of Mammon and the like. The lines recall the atmosphere of Isaiah 21:6–9, which envisions the fall of Babylon and all its 'graven images': '... set a watchman, let him declare what he seeth /.../ And he cried ... I stand continually upon the watchtower.../ And, behold, here cometh a chariot of men, with a couple of horsemen. And he answered and said, Babylon is fallen, is fallen ...'. Yet for all that the prophet in Isaiah 21 bewails his people's captivity, in this instance he does not anticipate the fall of Babylon – or *this* fall of Babylon – with relief.[9] Indeed he foresees it with foreboding: 'A grievous vision is declared unto me; the treacherous dealer dealeth treacherously, and the spoiler spoileth' (21:2). In 'All Along the Watchtower' the times may be changing, but apocalyptic powers of transformation may not be placeable within neat categories of either good or ill.

A comparable ambivalence of energy is the subject of 'Jokerman'. But where the questionable nature of joker and thief, as well as of riders and wind, is recounted in 'All Along the Watchtower' from something like a safe distance, by a speaker using the past tense, in 'Jokerman' a speaker addresses a figure identified as the Jokerman from the much less secure perspective of the present continuous. Throughout the lyric, no 'I' ever appears in apposition to the second person which is used in respect of the Jokerman. What we have is more a voice than a speaker: a disembodied voice that, rather than narrating a dialogue of the self from the outside, is directly involved in self-address, in a reflexive encounter with a principle of identity personified as Jokerman.

It is a principle defined in the lyric not by means of argument but through an accumulation – stanza by stanza – of images and attributions. The lyric proceeds by simultaneous repetition and amplification as each of its six verses introduces a fresh charge of images and perspectives. In the opening lines the Jokerman is a figure of preternatural capacity, a dispenser of spiritual sustenance in despite of the obdurate power of false gods:

That Forbidden Zone

> Standing on the waters casting your bread
> While the eyes of the idol with the iron head are glowing.

But it remains *in despite of*. The lines do not celebrate a delivery from or a victory over evil. There are, moreover, disturbances latent within the biblical echoes that haunt the first line. In Matthew 14:25 Christ is seen by his disciples 'walking on the sea', but it is Peter who loses faith as he walks 'on the water' (14:29) to meet his master: 'when he saw the wind boisterous, he was afraid; and beginning to sink, he cried, saying, Lord, save me' (14:30). Again, the injunction to fulfil the duty of beneficence in Ecclesiastes 11:1 – 'Cast thy bread upon the waters' – is set within a context (11:6) that affirms the uncertainty, even the inscrutability, of ultimate outcomes and ends: 'In the morning sow thy seed, and in the evening withhold not thine hand: for thou knowest not whether shall prosper, either this or that, or whether they shall both be alike good.' Despite his resources the Jokerman is subject to qualification and limitation. In the succeeding lines of the first stanza, the situation within which he is viewed is one of preparation for the ending of mortal life. Intimations of approaching death, of final release ('Distant ships...'; 'Freedom...'), intertwine with an emblematic evocation of a life of magisterial responsibility ('a snake in both of your fists').[10] But for all that death might be anticipated as a relief from the burdens of moral leadership, the inspired life-energy of the Jokerman ('hurricane...blowing') does not grant him absolute insight. Visions of the final end, of ultimate direction and purpose, are not vouchsafed:

> Distant ships sailing into the mist,
> You were born with a snake in both of your fists while a
>   hurricane was blowing.
> Freedom just around the corner for you
> But with the truth so far off, what good will it do?

That Forbidden Zone

The spiritual condition of the Jokerman remains equivocal throughout the lyric. Recurrently imaged as occupying a position removed from ordinary reality he is at the same time never envisaged as fully transcending that reality. His subjectivity is a site of incoherence, where contrasting elements and influences coincide without resolution. In the first lines of the fourth stanza, for example, opposite kinds of law meet in Jokerman: the strict codifications of moral order, on the one hand, and the amoral pulsions of nature, on the other:

> the Book of Leviticus and Deuteronomy,
> The law of the jungle and the sea are your only teachers.

In the projection of Jokerman in the following two lines of this verse, an affirmation of a pure harnessing of primal energy elides ambiguously with a glorification of libidinal drive. The Jokerman's medium is neither completely the light nor utterly the dark. And where there are possibilities of both a spiritual *and* an earthly potentate, of both a Christ-like grace *and* a humanist aggrandizement of the human, Michelangelo is aptly imagined as representing the ambivalence:

> In the smoke of the twilight on a milk-white steed,
> Michelangelo indeed could've carved out your features.

In the concluding lines of the fourth verse Jokerman is, as it were, suspended between dimensions, belonging wholly to none:

> Resting in the fields, far from the turbulent space,
> Half asleep near the stars with a small dog licking your face.

Indeterminacy is again the currency of the second stanza, which opens with hints of time running out and of the Jokerman passing above the attachments of this world:

> So swiftly the sun sets in the sky,
> You rise up and say goodbye to no one.

But while he may avoid foolish entanglement in worldly things, he does not ascend altogether to a higher plane. Neither the fear-filled future of the mortal fool nor the awe-ful destiny of an angel can be taken as the sole definition of his being or becoming:

> Fools rush in where angels fear to tread,
> Both of their futures, so full of dread, you don't show one.

Neither one nor the other, the principle of the Jokerman is in part founded on a tense inner relation between positive and negative potencies of identity. The second stanza ends with a picture of the Jokerman:

> Shedding off one more layer of skin,
> Keeping one step ahead of the persecutor within.

The irresolution of that stepping – the step ahead timed by and hence never finally clear of the step behind – is also the prevailing condition of the world through which the Jokerman moves. At the opening of the fifth verse:

> Well, the rifleman's stalking the sick and the lame,
> Preacherman seeks the same, who'll get there first is uncertain.

The inability of one term of a polarity to establish absolute priority over the other infects the gravest imaginings of 'Jokerman'. The speaking voice's conviction, at various points in the lyric, of an imminent threat to life in time posits a state outside time. But even the usableness of the opposition between time and non-time, life and death, is called into question in the final lines of stanza five as time – which from one point of view contrasts with death – is seen, with fine ironic understatement, as the very vehicle of death:

> False-hearted judges dying in the webs that they spin,
> Only a matter of time 'til night comes steppin' in.

Fraught with contrariety it is not surprising that the world of experience is envisaged in the lyric in terms of unreliable appearance. In the fifth stanza, 'Molotov cocktails and rocks behind every curtain', and in the sixth, 'It's a shadowy world, skies are slippery gray.' Nor is it only a matter of blurrings of definition. The lyric is also marked by images of the erasure of substance and form: 'Distant ships sailing into the mist.' It is a world in which things cannot be fixed and the Jokerman is himself repeatedly figured in images of obscuration ('In the smoke of the twilight') or effacement ('You rise up and say goodbye to no one'). Indeed the crucial problem with the oppositions and dualisms that go to constitute the nature of the Jokerman is that the relations between contrary terms are themselves never stabilized. At one level Jokerman has an aspect of grace that counterpoints the 'persecutor within'. But, more complexly, across the lyric as a whole, the principle of the Jokerman resists containment within a constant dualistic frame of reference. It is, instead, a principle of shifting quantities and values, a principle subject to multiform perspectives and with as many selves or potencies of self as there are skins to shed.

That Forbidden Zone

The last two lines of the third verse seem to define the Jokerman in consistently positive terms. Apparently a friend to the oppressed, he is also aware of the penalty paid by the rich man of Luke 16:19–31, who callously disregarded the poor in his life on earth:[11]

> Friend to the martyr, a friend to the woman of shame,
> You look into the fiery furnace, see the rich man without any name.

Yet this seemingly positive ascription is already undermined – albeit not cancelled out – by more disturbing elements in the characterization of Jokerman in the preceding four lines. Here there may again be traced, looked at one way, an extolling of the Jokerman's unworldliness and of his freedom to move in a fallen world because of his lack of ties with that world:

> You're a man of the mountains, you can walk on the clouds,
> Manipulator of crowds, you're a dream twister.
> You're going to Sodom and Gomorrah
> But what do you care? Ain't nobody there would want to marry your sister.

But even if we read the possibility of only a white magic in that capacity of spirit imaged in walking on clouds, it is hard to exclude the sinister aspect of the manipulation and twisting mentioned in the second line.

This troubling aspect of the Jokerman inheres in the various sources Dylan draws deeply upon in his projection of the Jokerman. There is, in the first place, the ancient type of the Jester, associated with the inversion of established – often specifically evil – rules and orders. Then there is the more

That Forbidden Zone

modern Joker of the playing-card pack. This is the odd card out, the potential trump that can take cards of any suit and which has power because its identity is variable, unpredictable. Related to the Jester and the precursor of the Joker in the pack is the Fool of the Tarot card set. Absorbed into Dylan's representation of his Jokerman is the typical design of the Tarot Fool as traversing a mountainous area – a small dog or feline animal biting at his legs – whilst blind to the abyss that opens up at his feet. J. E. Cirlot writes of the archetype of the Fool in the Tarot and elsewhere:

> The final enigma of the Tarot, distinguished from the others because it is un-numbered ... the significance of this is that the Fool is to be found on the fringe of all orders and systems. ... This figure on the Tarot card is dressed in a costume of many colours denoting the multiple or incoherent influences to which he is subject. ... This Tarot enigma corresponds, in short, to the irrational, the active instinct capable of sublimation, but related at the same time to blind impulse and the unconscious. ... [T]he mythic and legendary Fool is closely related to the clown. In their medicinal ceremonies and rites, doctor and patient 'act mad', and, through frenzied dancing and 'extravagances', they try to invert the prevailing evil order. The logic of the process is clear enough: when the normal or conscious appears to become infirm or perverted, in order to regain health and goodness it becomes necessary to turn to the dangerous, the unconscious and the abnormal.[12]

There may be a sacramental dimension to the figure of the Jester, Fool, Clown, or Joker. Subverting the daily order – apparently in touch with a spirituality beyond the material, or a creative energy drawing on imaginative spaces outside the logical and the syntactic – this figure *may* bear regenerative, redemptive potentialities. Its carnivalesque anarchism and irrationalism may be associated with a higher truth. Christ is sometimes figured as the Fool, in the same vein as St Paul observed that 'If any man among you seemeth to be wise in this world, let him become a fool, that he may be wise. / For the wisdom of this world is foolishness with God' (1 Corinthians 3:18-19). But in its distance from the containing structures of the world, in its subversive and transformational powers, the figure may at once elude fixture under the exclusive category of good. The space outside human systems which are predicated on difference and binary oppositions may not be chartable according to the terms of those differences and distinctions. The *ab*normal or the *un*conscious may be intimate with the dangerous and the dark as with the safe and the light. It may be a space conceivable either as full of a terrible paradox or as dreadfully empty of any kind of human meaning. In its transformations the Fool may transmute into the figure of the Trickster. The problem, in the nature of the case, is the undecidability of whether the Fool is in fact the Trickster. It is a problem caught again in that indeterminacy of sign which flickers through the opening stanza of 'Man of Peace', also from *Infidels*:

> Look out your window, baby, there's a scene you'd like to catch,
> The band is playing 'Dixie', a man got his hand outstretched.
> Could be the Führer
> Could be the local priest.
> You know sometimes Satan comes as a man of peace.

In 'Jokerman', are the Christological stature of the figure that stands on water and walks on clouds, and the mystical exaltation of the man of the mountains, evidences of an authentic and authenticated spiritual capacity, evidences of access to some form of verifiable higher authority? Or are they the manipulative twists – the shams, the illusions – of a charlatan, a joker?

That Forbidden Zone

Comparably, the Jokerman's unconcernedness at engaging a fallen world may be a symptom of having risen above fallen nature, but it may signify a culpable disregard. 'But what do you care?' Is he without the care of the world or is he uncaring? And if not an active disregard, there remains a question about the quality of even an authentic spirituality that, in gazing beyond this world, is careless of the travails of this world. Is it a carelessness transfigured by its attention to an absolute that providentially guarantees the world's rescue? Or is the temporal remoteness of such a promised, consummatory rescue something that involves the spiritual gaze in a type of violence against the world with all its immediate problems? Equally, what are the implications for a suffering world if the absolute object of spiritual contemplation is an object that altogether eludes good and bad, positive and negative discriminations?

Nor is the reflexive voice of the lyric easier to position than the principle it addresses. 'But what do you care?' The stance and tone of the question might be collusively endorsing or they might be accusing. Similarly with 'You rise up and say goodbye to no one' in the second stanza. A laudable religious detachment or an irresponsibility towards the common human pieties? The problematics of the Jokerman principle turn on the fact that if there is something void or negative here it is not distinguishable from what can at the same time appear a replete and graceful potentiality.

The questions are brought to a head, though not to an answer, in the final stanza of 'Jokerman', where the Jokerman is envisaged in relation to an *apparent* agency of evil:

It's a shadowy world, skies are slippery gray,
A woman just gave birth to a prince today and dressed him in scarlet.
He'll put the priest in his pocket, put the blade to the heat,

> Take the motherless children off the street
> And place them at the feet of a harlot.
> Oh, Jokerman, you know what he wants,
> Oh, Jokerman, you don't show any response.[13]

Does he want opposition, submission, co-operation, or indifference? And is the lack of response a form of opposition, of submission, of co-operation, or of indifference? The matter remains potently open. As open as the questions Dylan had put twenty years earlier in the 1963 'Blowin' in the Wind' (*The Freewheelin' Bob Dylan*). 'How many seas must a white dove sail / Before she sleeps in the sand?'; or, 'how many times can a man turn his head, / Pretending he just doesn't see?' The answer then had been such as to raise only more questions: 'The answer, my friend, is blowin' in the wind.' Likewise, 'Jokerman' dictates no response other than a question to its image of a lack of response and the lyric remains unclosed by a refrain which registers a dancing in time that is at once a dance of death and a flight of the soul by a light that governs both creativity and waste:[14]

> Jokerman dance to the nightingale tune,
> Bird fly high by the light of the moon...

In 'Jokerman' Dylan adopts the figure of the Joker to give emblematic shape to a vision of the bizarre, undecidable nature of human identity. Generating questions which it does not resolve, the lyric itself is presented to its audience in the form of a question or riddle. In its refusal to close lies its strength, its commitment to confront and challenge. And in that refusal it epitomizes the most distinctive perspective of Dylan's lyrical career: a continually renewed scepticism regarding the possibility of attaining absolutely final positions and a protest at the paralysing intolerance of such as settle for closed and fixed points of view. The work neither simply despairs nor simply celebrates. Recognizing a 'hateful siege / Of contraries'[15] it simultaneously exults in that siege. For it is only in the relative state of which it speaks that the lyric is itself constituted and can beat out its own rhythmic and rhyming time. 'Jokerman' marks time ('Keeping one step ahead . . .'; 'a matter of time 'til night comes steppin' . . .') in a realm where truth might, though it might not, lie just around the corner. Affirming the resilience necessary to leaving things in play, the lyric bears witness to the bleak and exhilarating necessity of holding things in play, to the fundamentally unavoidable dynamic of 'not *stopping*'.[16]

Appendix
Chronology of Dylan's Career and Officially Released Recordings

Song-lyrics discussed in length in the preceding chapters are marked with an asterisk under the album on which they appear.

1941 (24 May) Born (Robert Allen Zimmerman) in Duluth, Minnesota. The Zimmermans move to Hibbing, Minnesota, when Dylan is six.

1959 (September) Dylan enrolls at the University of Minnesota, Minneapolis, frequenting the nearby Bohemian district and singing in a coffee house, the Ten O'Clock Scholar. Of this period Dylan recalls in conversation:

> I came out of the wilderness and just naturally fell in with the beat scene.... there was a lot of unrest in the country. You could feel it, a lot of frustration, sort of like a calm before a hurricane, things were shaking up. ... There were a lot of poets and painters, drifters, scholarly types, experts at one thing or another who had dropped out of the regular nine-to-five life, there were a lot of house parties most of the time.... a girlfriend of mine in New York, later turned me on to all the French poets but for then it was Jack Kerouac, Ginsberg, Corso and Ferlinghetti.... America was still very 'straight', 'post-war' and sort of into a gray-flannel suit thing, McCarthy, commies, puritanical, very claustrophobic and whatever was happening

of any real value was happening away from that and sort of hidden from view and it would be years before the media would be able to recognize it and choke-hold it and reduce it to silliness. Anyway, I got in at the tail-end of that and it was magic ... Pound, Camus, T. S. Eliot, e.e. cummings ... Burroughs, John Rechy, Gary Snyder ... the newer poets and folk music, jazz, Monk, Coltrane, Sonny and Brownie, Big Bill Broonzy, Charlie Christian ... it all left the rest of everything in the dust ... I knew I had to get to New York though, I'd been dreaming about that for a long time.[1]

1960 (December) Sets out for New York.

1961 (January) Arrives in New York. Visits Woody Guthrie – doyen of American Depression song-writers – in New Jersey hospital.

(January–April) Frequents New Left and folk music circles, playing small clubs such as the Gaslight, in the coffee house society of Greenwich Village. 'He began ... immediately ... to find admirers. The admiration was by no means universal, however, for even at that time, Dylan's trademark elusiveness made him hard to place. He wasn't traditional.... He certainly wasn't commercial – his voice was at once hoarse and nasal, his mumble sometimes impenetrable.'[2]

(April) First professional appearance at central Greenwich Village venue, Gerde's Folk City, supporting bluesman John Lee Hooker.

(June) First work in recording studio: commissioned to play harmonica on Harry Belafonte's album, *Midnight Special*. Frustrated by the demand for repeated retakes of the same performance, Dylan leaves the recording sessions. Unimportant in itself, the episode signals crucial features of Dylan's performative mode throughout his career: an unwillingness to sing a song exactly the same way twice and a resistance to the exigencies of commercial finish or gloss. The risks run in respect of both concert and studio performance (Dylan's studio albums are characteristically recorded in relatively short periods of time) are high. But against the losses, the turning in of weak or poorly produced performances, the gains are performances of an unprogrammeable strength.

(October–November) Signs contract with CBS and records material for first album.

1962 (March) *Bob Dylan*. This first album has two original Dylan compositions. The remainder of the record, including versions of songs by Jesse Fuller, Bukka White and Blind Lemon Jefferson, shows Dylan in the process of assimilating and redirecting blues and traditional folk registers.

(May) 'Blowin' in the Wind' printed in *Broadside* – an early type of the 1960s underground press committed to publishing alternative and 'topical' song lyrics. 'Blowin' in the Wind' came to be adopted as a Civil Rights movement anthem and did perhaps more to establish Dylan than any other single song.

(August) Changes name legally. Dylan had been using his adopted name regularly since at least 1959.

(September) Writes 'A Hard Rain's A-Gonna Fall', a lyric of apocalyptic resonance (at points almost a pastiche of the number symbolism of the Book of Revelation) apposite to the atmosphere surrounding the Cuban missile crisis of 1962.

1963 (April) First major solo concert appearance, Town Hall, New York City.

Appendix

(May) Dylan walks out of CBS-TV's *Ed Sullivan Show* after being refused permission to sing 'Talkin' John Birch Paranoid Blues', a talking blues lyric (never officially released on record) satirizing the extreme right-wing John Birch Society.

(May) *The Freewheelin' Bob Dylan*. Includes both 'Blowin' in the Wind' and 'A Hard Rains A-Gonna Fall' and also such songs as 'Masters of War' and 'Talkin' World War III Blues' (a caustically humorous dream-vision of the conditions of nuclear war). The album addresses – though not exclusively – issues of social and political relevance.

(July) Dylan sings with Joan Baez during his first performance at Newport Folk Festival.

(August) Sings at Civil Rights march on Washington led by Martin Luther King, Jr.

(December) Dylan receives Tom Paine Award of the Emergency Civil Liberties Committee. At the presentation ceremony Dylan scandalizes the audience by saying that he could see in himself some of the things that had driven Lee Harvey Oswald to shoot President John F. Kennedy (on 22 November). The incident serves as an index of Dylan's rejection of one-dimensional social and psychological frames of reference ('They actually thought I was saying it was a good thing Kennedy had been killed').[3]

1964 (January) *The Times They are A-Changin'*. Notable for its social and political songs, including 'The Times They are A-Changin'', 'Ballad of Hollis Brown', 'With God On Our Side', 'Only a Pawn in Their Game' and 'The Lonesome Death of Hattie Carroll', the last a consummately realized piece concerned with the murder of a Baltimore waitress.

Chronology of Dylan's Career

(May) Performs at Royal Festival Hall, London.

(July) Introduces 'Mr. Tambourine Man' at Newport Folk Festival.

(August) *Another Side of Bob Dylan*. Marks an emphasis away from what Dylan termed 'finger-pointing songs'.[4] Numerous lyrics concentrate on personal relationships. The entrapments of certain types of doctrinaire position, right or left, are explored in 'My Back Pages', 'Chimes of Freedom', 'Motorpsycho Nightmare' and 'I Shall Be Free No. 10'. The last mocks naïve liberalism as – alluding to an Arizona politician and invoking in reverse two clichés of racist feeling – it points out that liberalism itself needs must practise repression: 'Now, I'm liberal, but to a degree / I want ev'rybody to be free / But if you think that I'll let Barry Goldwater / Move in next door and marry my daughter / You must think I'm crazy! / I wouldn't let him do it for all the farms in Cuba.' Dylan's social and political lyrics had rarely been one-sided or monotonal but *Another Side of Bob Dylan*, confirming tendencies apparent at the Newport Folk Festival a month before, provoked hostile reaction from Dylan's first guard of support. A *Broadside* column in December was to speak bitterly of 'the renunciation of topical music by its major prophet'.

(October) Performs at Philharmonic Hall, New York, incorporating songs – 'Mr. Tambourine Man', 'Gates of Eden', 'It's All Right, Ma (I'm Only Bleeding)' – that were to appear the following Spring on *Bringing It All Back Home*.

1965   (January) Recording sessions for *Bringing It All Back Home*. The material on this album marks Dylan's decisive movement into a lyric mode characterized by indirection

149

and obscurity – a mode dominating, in different forms, not only *Bringing It All Back Home* but Dylan's three other outstanding albums of the 1960s, *Highway 61 Revisited* (1965), *Blonde on Blonde* (1966) and *John Wesley Harding* (1968).

(March) *Bringing it All Back Home*

'Subterranean Homesick Blues' / *"She Belongs to Me' / 'Maggie's Farm' / *"Love Minus Zero/No Limit' / 'Outlaw Blues' / 'On The Road Again' / 'Bob Dylan's 115th Dream' / *"Mr. Tambourine Man' / 'Gates of Eden' / 'It's Alright, Ma (I'm Only Bleeding)' / *"It's All Over Now, Baby Blue'.

In addition to the interiority of much of the lyrical writing, this album also marks – in the use of electrified instruments on several of its cuts – Dylan's transition from acoustic to rock music. The title *Bringing It All Back Home* hinted in part at a wresting of musical initiative from British performers at that time spearheading a revival of blues-based rock. One of the major influences on the electric elements of the album was the black lead guitarist Bruce Langhorne. 'By all accounts, the *Bringing It All Back Home* sessions were typical Dylan chaos, but to the extent that they can be said to have had an arranger other than Dylan himself, it was Langhorne.'[5] *Bringing It All Back Home*'s peculiar contribution, however, lay in its conjunction of lyric sophistication with electronic musical backing. With this album Dylan 'began sucessfully to reinvigorate rock with his emotionally evocative, vituperative, and surrealistic song poetics ... vastly expanding the concepts and concerns of contemporary ... song writing. ... whereas The Beatles were establishing the album as the unit of public consumption of music, Dylan was establishing the album as the unit of personal ... expression.'[6]

(April–May) Concert tour in Britain, concluding at the Royal Albert Hall, London. This tour is the subject of the D. A. Pennebaker *cinema verité* film *Don't Look Back*.

(June) 'Like a Rolling Stone', later issued on *Highway 61 Revisited*, is released as a single and is instrumental in confirming Dylan's capacity to reach beyond 'folk' circles to a mass rock audience. At six minutes the song 'permanently broke the recording industry's 3-minute song-length rule';[7] 'Perhaps most important, though, it opened the range of "natural voice" possibilities that would be available to subsequent performers.'[8]

(July) Dylan provokes ill-feeling at the Newport Folk Festival as he plays with electronic backing provided by the Paul Butterfield Blues Band. Newport 1965 occupies a place of special significance both in the context of Dylan's career (the episode is a talisman of Dylan's recurrent challenging of audience expectation) and in terms of the development of rock music as a whole. Dylan 'led the movement towards serious lyrical content in rock and roll music'[9] and Newport 1965 is the symbolic focus of that movement's initial impetus. In August 1987 the *Economist* reviewed the tenth anniversary commemorations – at his former home Graceland – of Elvis Presley's death, together with a book by Chicago University professor Allan Bloom (*The Closing of the American Mind*) decrying the mass rock music culture that had been initiated by Presley in the mid-1950s:

What is missing, in Mr Bloom's book as elsewhere, is any explanation ... of how largely innocent dance music became

Appendix

within ten years a backing-track for the social and intellectual whirlwind of the 1960s. Curiously, the answer seems to lie on Mr Bloom's own doorstep.

The University of Chicago ... sits like a placid island in the wasteland of Chicago's South Side. All around it, from the 1940s on, black immigrants from the Mississippi Delta electrified their folk music and turned it into a unique, driving urban blues.

In the early 1960s, Paul Butterfield, a white student at the University, decided that he wanted to play the blues too, and did. His band of white and black musicians got a terrific local following. In 1965, the Butterfield band was invited to play at the annual Newport Folk Festival in Rhode Island. Folk was, with jazz, the music of café society intellectuals.

Their hero was Mr Bob Dylan, who accompanied himself on the acoustic guitar. At Newport, Mr Dylan asked the Butterfield band to back him with their loud electrified instruments. The audience was enraged; Mr Pete Seeger, the doyen of folk, is said to have tried to disconnect the amplifiers.

After the concert, Mr Dylan turned his back on his old audience and moved towards rock. But he lost none of his intellectual pretensions along the way. Ever after, rock would be about a lot more than hot cars, ponytails and teenage love. Mr Dylan's switch to electrified music was a seminal moment in the loss of that American cultural innocence celebrated at Graceland....

On Dylan's use of electrified instruments, Geoffrey Stokes has observed that:

In a ... burst of innovation ... an entire new genre of white pop was ... created by a merger of the folkies' outsider intellectualism with the newly revivified energies of rock. At the center of this development – as writer, performer, arbiter of the scene – stood Bob Dylan.... When he 'went electric', he simply carried the homemade aspects of folkie recording along with him, and none of his records ever achieved – or even aimed for – the standard industry level of studio gloss.... Except, perhaps, for the early, pre-tamed Elvis, there really wasn't a musical antecedent.... Once Dylan's folkie audience started to merge with the Beatles', it started asking 'Why can't *they* do that? Are they (dread word) superficial?'.... Dylan ... had created a revolution of rising expectations.[10]

(August) Repeated antagonism to electronic backing during concert at Forest Hills Stadium, New York.

Dylan had done an acoustic set for the first half of the show, for which he received a standing ovation, and then returned with his then band (Al Kooper, Harvey Brooks, Levon Helm, and Robbie Robertson) after intermission. As Kooper recalled: '... we got ready to go out and do the second part as an electric band. Then Bob took us to one side. "It's gonna be very weird out there", he said, "... anything could happen ... I just want you to know that"....

Well, we played the first thirty seconds, and the audience just started booing.... Then people started rushing the stage to grab him, and I got knocked over ... he just stood there, with the wind blowing his hair out sideways ... and the booing went on....'

Kooper has described himself as amazed by Dylan's reaction at the postconcert party – he 'walked right over and hugged me. "Wasn't it fantastic?" he said. He was really happy about it'....[11]

(August) *Highway 61 Revisited*
'Like a Rolling Stone' / 'Tombstone Blues' / 'It Takes a Lot to Laugh, It Takes a Train to Cry' / 'From a Buick Six' / *'Ballad of a Thin Man' / 'Queen Jane Approximately' /

Appendix

'Highway 61 Revisited' / 'Just Like Tom Thumb's Blues' / *'Desolation Row'.

This album – its lyric intensities charged with vocal and musical anger – consolidates Dylan's movement into rock and his command of a new audience. 'Critics were positively shocked by ... *Highway 61 Revisted*. ... The album, recorded with Mike Bloomfield on electric guitar and Al Kooper on keyboards, created an unmistakeable sound and featured some of Dylan's most startling songwriting.'[12]

(September–December) First part of North American leg of world tour. Beginning with a concert at Hollywood Bowl, Los Angeles, the tour will continue, with few sustained breaks, to May 1966.

1966 (February–April) Continuation of North American leg followed by Australian leg of world tour. Dylan's refusal of encroachments by the media is highlighted during the course of this tour, conducted in the wake of controversy about his rock settings. What have remained Dylan's modes of resistance – ranging from a dourly monosyllabic inarticulacy through deliberate misinformation to impatient ridicule – are markedly apparent. Interviewed in March:

Q. '... what made you decide to go the rock 'n' roll route?'
A. 'Carelessness. I lost my one true love. I started drinking. The first thing I know, I'm in a card game. Then I'm in a crap game. I wake up in a pool hall. Then this big Mexican lady drags me off the table, takes me to Philadelphia. She leaves me alone in her house, and it burns down. I wind up in Phoenix. I get a job as a Chinaman. I start working in a dime store, and move in with a thirteen-year-old girl.

Then this big Mexican lady from Philadelphia comes in and burns the house down. I go down to Dallas. I get a job as a 'before' in a Charles Atlas 'before and after' ad. I move in with a delivery boy who can cook fantastic chilli and hot dogs. Then this thirteen-year-old girl from Phoenix comes and burns the house down. The delivery boy – he ain't so mild: he gives her the knife, and the next thing I know I'm in Omaha. It's so cold there, by this time I'm robbing my own bicycles and frying my own fish. I stumble onto some luck and get a job as a carburetter out at the hot-rod races every Thursday night. I move in with a high school teacher who also does a little plumbing on the side, who ain't much to look at, but who's built a special kind of refrigerator that can turn newspaper into lettuce. Everything's going good until that delivery boy shows up and tries to knife me: Needless to say, he burned the house down, and I hit the road. The first guy that picked me up asked me if I wanted to be a star. What could I say?'[13]

(April–May) European leg of world tour. Dylan encounters delayed European version of antagonism towards shifts of emphasis in his lyrics and music ('Judas!', called a member of an audience in Britain: Dylan responded, 'I don't believe you ... you're a liar'). Robbie Robertson of the backing group (later The Band) would remember: 'That tour was a very strange process. You can hear the violence, and the dynamics in the music. We'd go from town to town, from country to country.... We set up, we played, they booed and threw things at us. Then we went to the next town, played, they booed, threw things, and we left again.'[14] The tour highlights the manner in which Dylan's occupation of an adversarial position in relation to his audience is the condition of some of his finest performances. *Eat the Document*, a film edited by Dylan

Appendix

and Howard Alk and publicly screened on only a few occasions, records sequences of the tour.

(May) *Blonde on Blonde*

'Rainy Day Women Nos. 12 & 35' / 'Pledging My Time' / *'Visions of Johanna' / 'One of Us Must Know (Sooner or Later)' / 'I Want You' / 'Stuck Inside of Mobile with the Memphis Blues Again' / 'Leopard-Skin Pill-Box Hat' / 'Just Like a Woman' / 'Most Likely You Go Your Way (and I'll Go Mine)' / 'Temporary Like Achilles' / 'Absolutely Sweet Marie' / 'Fourth Time Around' / 'Obviously Five Believers' / 'Sad-Eyed Lady of the Lowlands'.

The lyric obliquities of this album fuse with what Dylan later characterized as its 'thin. . . . wild mercury sound'.[15] '*Blonde on Blonde*, probably the first non-anthology double-record set by a major contemporary artist, revealed an unprecedented level of performance and lyrical invention';[16] 'wild, trippy . . . obscure' (*Listener*).

(July) Dylan has motorcycle accident, suffering concussion and cracked vertebrae in his neck. Following the accident, Dylan continued releasing records but was to make very few public appearances for nearly eight years.

1967 (March) *Bob Dylan's Greatest Hits*. Essentially a standard record industry compilation.

(June–October) Dylan writes, plays and records in private sessions with members of The Band. Some of the results of these sessions were to appear officially in 1975 on *The Basement Tapes*. Many appeared unofficially much earlier. These unofficial recordings were a major initiative behind the development of the illegal bootleg industry, which rapidly expanded to embrace the work of other rock performers. There exist many hundreds of bootleg

Chronology of Dylan's Career

recordings of private or studio sessions and concert performances by Dylan, ranging from the earliest New York days to the present time. Among these are many performances of songs that have substantial lyrical as well as musical variations from the officially released versions, together with numerous songs never officially released by Dylan (though in some cases the lyric texts are printed in *Lyrics, 1962-1985*).[17]

1968 (January) *John Wesley Harding*

'John Wesley Harding' / 'As I Went Out One Morning' / 'I Dreamed I Saw St. Augustine' / *'All Along The Watchtower' / 'The Ballad of Frankie Lee and Judas Priest' / 'Drifter's Escape' / 'Dear Landlord' / 'I Am a Lonesome Hobo' / 'I Pity the Poor Immigrant' / 'The Wicked Messenger' / 'Down Along the Cove' / 'I'll Be Your Baby Tonight'.

Setting itself against the electronic elaboration which had overtaken studio records since 1966, this album fits parabolically insinuating lyrics to a musical base defined by a minimum of instrumentation. 'Flinty music...full of savage melancholy' (*London Magazine*). '[T]he album would have been understated even by the standards of 1964. In January 1968, it was as though Dylan had flung open the window of an overheated room....'[18]

(January) Dylan performs at Carnegie Hall, New York, in benefit concerts commemorating the death, in October 1967, of Woody Guthrie.

1969 (April) *Nashville Skyline*. A collection of country style songs, for the most part pointedly slight in lyric content and delivered in a mellow voice rarely heard elsewhere in Dylan's work. Of the most distinctive piece, Frank

157

Appendix

Kermode observes: 'How different from the characteristically rebarbative whine is the baritone assurance of "Lay, Lady, Lay". This song also has a very accomplished lyric: no explanations, but enough suggestiveness. . . . to keep it clear of the banality of pop love song.'[19] *Nashville Skyline* – with its studied disengagement from either political stance or lyric complexity – provoked consternation among sections of Dylan's audience. For many, in retrospect, it ushered in a low period in Dylan's creative career which was to last until his North American tour of 1974 and the release in 1975 of *Blood on the Tracks*.

(August) Performs in England at the Isle of Wight Music Festival, having declined to preside over the 'Woodstock' Festival at Bethel, New York, a few weeks earlier.

1970 (June) *Self Portrait*. A collection of twenty-four songs, of which a large proportion are not Dylan's own compositions but his interpretations of a variety of traditional folk, blues, or popular pieces, including a version of the Rodgers and Hart 'Blue Moon'. Dylan's interest in sometimes performing other people's songs has remained consistent throughout his career. Some responses to *Self Portrait* saw the collection primarily in the light of this interest. Others saw in the album an extension of the implicit statement of *Nashville Skyline*: a typically Dylanesque resistance to audience expectation, including the expectation that he write politically or poetically significant songs. Generally, however, *Self Portrait* was received with bewilderment and hostility as a further evidence, along with *Nashville Skyline*, of Dylan's betrayal of his own powers. Nor was the irony of the album title sufficient to deflect scathing diagnoses of Dylan as creatively exhausted. The opening line of a review in *Rolling Stone*: 'What is this shit?'

(June) Receives honorary Doctorate of Music at Princeton University.

(October) *New Morning*. Songs of simple pleasure ('New Morning') mix with songs of repressed tension, such as 'Went to See the Gypsy' and Dylan's first jazz-song, 'If Dogs Run Free', which sets the lyric voice against what Frank Kermode calls 'the delicious wordless vocal scribble of a black scat-singer'.[20]

1971 (May) *Tarantula*. A sequence of prose pieces originally written by Dylan in the mid-1960s, and published in response to widespread unauthorized circulation of the work.

(August) Dylan contributes to George Harrison's benefit Concert for Bangladesh at Madison Square Garden, New York. Performances by Dylan appear on both the record and the film entitled *The Concert for Bangladesh*.

(November) *Bob Dylan's Greatest Hits, Vol. 2*. For the most part a standard record industry compilation, but has a number of previously unreleased songs, including 'When I Paint My Masterpiece' (1971 recording) and *'I Shall be Released' (1971 recording of a work dating from Dylan's June–October 1967 sessions with members of The Band; reissued on *Biograph*).

1972 (November–December) Dylan takes part in the filming of Sam Peckinpah's *Pat Garrett and Billy the Kid*, playing a cameo role as 'Alias' and composing the music for the film soundtrack. Work on the set will continue through January and February of the following year, the completed film being released in May.

Appendix

1973 (July) *Pat Garrett and Billy the Kid*. Film soundtrack.

(November) *Dylan*. An album of ephemeral studio out-takes, none of them original Dylan compositions, apparently released by CBS during a period of contractual disagreement between Dylan and the record company. 'The most embarrassing piece of plastic ever released in the name of a great artist' (*Guardian*).

Writings and Drawings by Bob Dylan, gathering (though not exhaustively) Dylan's lyrics to 1971, is first published by Knopf this year.

1974 (January) *Planet Waves*. Has a number of discreetly barbed lyrics, including 'On a Night Like This', 'Something There Is About You', and 'Forever Young'.

(January–February) Undertakes with The Band a forty date North American concert tour. Opening in Chicago, Dylan's first tour since 1966 attracts some five million ticket applications for a total of 650,000 seats ('The biggest financial response for any event in entertainment history,' noted *Melody Maker*). From its inception the tour is greeted as a triumphant return: 'Suddenly the blue spot streaked out through the drifting smoke ... and in the vivid blue pool on the stage the man was flooded in colour – smallish, spindly ... with old boots and a rough cloth jacket ... and with a harmonica perched on a strangely cantilevered neckstrap.... The sound that broke with the light was like Chicago tearing in half.... The sound went on and on until the spindly little man picked up his guitar and turned to his five companions with a nod and the first notes crashed out. Bob Dylan, after eight long years on the cold outside, was back on the road again' (*Guardian*); 'Dylan gained a whole new audience' (*New Musical Express*). The energy of the tour presages Dylan's concentrated activity throughout the remainder of the 1970s, with further major concert tours and four outstanding studio albums: *Blood on the Tracks* (1975), *Desire* (1976), *Street Legal* (1978), and *Slow Train Coming* (1979).

(May) Performs at Felt Forum, Madison Square Garden, in a benefit concert organized by the Friends of Chile for refugees from the junta that deposed Socialist president Salvador Allende.

(June) *Before the Flood*. A double album of live performances by Dylan and by The Band from the tour of January–February.

1975 (January) *Blood on the Tracks*

*'Tangled Up in Blue' / 'Simple Twist of Fate' / 'You're a Big Girl Now' / 'Idiot Wind' / 'You're Gonna Make Me Lonesome When You Go' / 'Meet Me in the Morning' / 'Lily, Rosemary and the Jack of Hearts' / 'If You See Her, Say Hello' / *'Shelter from the Storm' / 'Buckets of Rain'.

Elaborate explorations of narrative structure constitute one of the major achievements of this collection of songs. '*Blood on the Tracks* ... marks yet another change in [Dylan's] mood and style.... Musically, the overall mood is relaxed and melodic, with the all-out rock or country influences giving way to a rhythmic, acoustic style – strummed guitars, harmonica, organ and bass. Lyrically, though, the changes are drastic.... To say there's blood on these tracks is something of an indulgent overstatement.... Yet ... it does seem that a degree of pain helps [Dylan's] writing. ... the finest track of all, an extraordinary outburst called 'Idiot Wind' ... piled up with ... surreal imagery and hints of influences back to Woody Guthrie ... can be taken as an all-purpose anthem against

Appendix

mediocrity in the media and the collapse of American idealism' (*Guardian*).

(July) *The Basement Tapes*. Sixteen Dylan songs (with other material performed by The Band) from the June–October 1967 sessions with members of The Band, recorded on non-studio equipment in the basement of The Band's house, Big Pink, near Woodstock. The imaginative force of many of the Dylan lyrics (including 'This Wheel's On Fire', 'Tears of Rage'), and the raucous and sometimes grim humour of others (including 'Please, Mrs. Henry', 'Million Dollar Bash'), combines with a raw spontaneity in performance and production.

(July) Dylan begins frequenting Greenwich Village for the first time in many years, participating in performances at such clubs as the Bottom Line (with Muddy Waters) and the Other End (with Patti Smith). The idea of a distinctive kind of tour – ultimately mounted in October and titled the Rolling Thunder Revue – takes shape during the course of this summer.

(October–December) The first phase of the Rolling Thunder Revue – undertaking generally unannounced performances at a mixture of small to middle-sized venues – tours the north-eastern United States and Canada. The variable troupe accompanying Dylan include: Mick Ronson, Scarlet Rivera, T-Bone Burnette, Ronee Blakeley, Roger McGuinn, Jack Elliott, Joan Baez, Allen Ginsberg, Peter Orlovsky, Lou Kemp, Jacques Levy, David Blue, Bob Neuwirth, Roberta Flack, Sam Shepard. The tenor of the tour is one of secrecy, to avoid the commercial paraphernalia of the standard rock tour, and of improvisation – 'like a travelling vaudeville show or a travelling circus – the jugglers and the clowns ... no tuning up between songs... no pauses'.[21] Dylan alludes to the *Commedia dell'Arte* in his conception of a show which – making much use of mask and costume – does not simply perform at audiences but is actively involved in exploring within itself character roles and types.[22] In his journal of the tour Sam Shepard notes some of the archetypes and personae invoked by the Revue: 'Alchemist / Magician / Preacher / Poet / Teacher / Medicine Man / Wizard / Saint / Demon / Witch / Gunfighter / Boxer / Prophet / Thief / Cowboy / Devil / Assassin / Bride / Lover / Truck Driver / Pilgrim / King / Emperor / Fisherman / Drifter / Messenger / A Nobody / Priest / Queen / Shaman / Idiot'.[23] At the start of the following year *Rolling Stone* was to write of the Revue: 'From a myth-making point of view this is all astonishingly effective stuff. Here a man does a limited tour... refusing to make known his itinerary, doesn't release an album, does no interviews, is actively hostile to what little press penetrates his defenses – and winds up with extraordinary amounts of acclaim and attention.' Dylan used the attention to highlight a cause with which he was preoccupied during the tour: the case of Rubin 'Hurricane' Carter, a black middleweight boxer who had served nine years of a life prison sentence for a multiple murder in Paterson, New Jersey, in 1966. Dylan lent his support to a campaign for Carter's retrial, releasing as a single in November the song 'Hurricane' (which accuses the police and key prosecution witnesses of having lied) and bringing the first phase of the Rolling Thunder Revue to a climax in December with a benefit concert for the Carter campaign at Madison Square Garden. A second benefit concert for the Carter campaign was held in the Houston Astrodome, Texas, in January. In the same month Carter

Appendix

was released on bail pending a retrial which a year later again found him guilty. In November 1985 this second conviction was overturned by a Federal Judge.

1976 (January) *Desire*

'Hurricane' / *'Isis' / 'Mozambique' / 'One More Cup of Coffee (Valley Below)' / 'Oh, Sister' / 'Joey' / 'Romance in Durango' / 'Black Diamond Bay' / 'Sara'.

The collection is distinguished by its exploration of psychological and familial archetypes. 'One of the reasons [*Desire*] is so good is a ... lady violinist called Scarlet Rivera. ... she provides a slithering urgent accompaniment to Dylan's voice, matching him with ... understanding and imagination' (*Guardian*).

(April–May) Second phase of the Rolling Thunder Revue, touring outside the north-eastern United States and differing somewhat in format and tone from the first phase, not least in its concentration on larger venues.

(September) *Hard Rain*. Live performances from the second phase of the Rolling Thunder Revue. A television film – entitled *Hard Rain* – of Dylan's performances in May at Fort Collins, Colorado, is also shown in the United States this month. '*Hard Rain*, the ... television special, gave ... an hour-long abridgement of a rain-drenched stadium concert. ... the songs, the arrangements ... the manner of presentation ... seemed to give everybody something to complain about. ... *He didn't even talk!* ... Dylan hadn't realized that when you are a visitor in the living room of America, you have to make small talk, keep your hands on your lap, and not make threats' (*Free Times*, Philadelphia).

(November) Contributes to The Band's farewell concert at the Winterland Palace, San Francisco. Part of Dylan's

Chronology of Dylan's Career

performance is included in the record of the concert, *The Last Waltz*; and a part is included in the Martin Scorsese film of the concert, *The Last Waltz*, both released in April 1978.

1978 (January) *Renaldo and Clara*. Four-hour film directed by Dylan and composed largely of concert, documentary and extemporized dramatic scenes shot during the first phase of The Rolling Thunder Revue at the end of 1975. Preoccupied with questions of identity the film examines the nature of different kinds of discourse and breaks down strict separations between the fictional and non-fictional. On the construction of the film Allen Ginsberg comments:

What he did was, he shot about 110 hours of film, or more, and he looked at it all. Then he put it all on index cards, according to some preconceptions he had when he was directing and shooting. Namely, themes: God, rock and roll, art, poetry, marriage, women, sex, Bob Dylan, poets, death – maybe eighteen or twenty thematic preoccupations. Then he also put on index cards all the different characters, all the scenes. He also marked on index cards the dominant colour – blue or red ... and certain other images that go through the movie, like the rose and the hat, and Indians – American Indians – so that he finally had an index of all that.

And then he went through it all again and began composing it, thematically, weaving in and out of those specific compositional references.

So it's compositional, and the idea was not to have a plot, but to have a composition of those themes.[24]

Renaldo and Clara was not well received ('It is ... difficult to understand why a man of his sensibilities has allowed such a hotchpotch of unfinished, rambling jumble to

Appendix

appear under his name', *The Times*; 'incredibly boring', *New Musical Express*). Exemption was, however, made for the sequences of concert footage. Many of Dylan's performances during the first phase of the Rolling Thunder Revue were charged with a peculiar intensity and the film provides an invaluable record of such performances.

(February–April) Japanese and Australian leg of world tour that will last through to December, comprising some 115 concerts.

(February) *Masterpieces*. Released initially in Japan and subsequently in Australia and New Zealand, a triple album retrospective collection including some live performances of songs and some pieces either previously unreleased or released only as singles.

(June–July) European leg of world tour. Dylan's first concert appearance in Britain for nine years sells out 100,000 seats at Earl's Court concerts, London, in June. Dylan returns to Britain in July to end the European tour with a concert at Blackbushe Aerodrome, Surrey, playing to some 200,000 people (the biggest audience for a rock concert in Britain since the Isle of Wight festival in 1969).

(June) *Street Legal*

'Changing of the Guards' / *'New Pony' / 'No Time to Think' / 'Baby, Stop Crying' / 'Is Your Love in Vain?' / 'Señor (Tales of Yankee Power)' / 'True Love Tends to Forget' / 'We Better Talk This Over' / 'Where Are You Tonight? (Journey Through Dark Heat)'.

One of Dylan's lyrically most experimental collections. Several of the most richly complex songs on the album (notably 'Changing of the Guards') look forward to the Christian perspectives Dylan was to assume on his next studio album, *Slow Train Coming*.

(November) *Bob Dylan at Budokan*. A double album of live performances from the opening Japanese section of the 1978 world tour, released initially in Japan. Gives a good indication of the new rock arrangements of many old songs which Dylan introduced on this tour, though some reviewers regretted that a live album had not been released which drew on later stages of the tour when, they felt, performances had gained in depth and power. Other reviewers simply regretted the new arrangements.

(September–December) North American leg of world tour.

1979 (August) *Slow Train Coming*

'Gotta Serve Somebody' / *'Precious Angel' / 'I Believe in You' / 'Slow Train' / 'Gonna Change My Way of Thinking' / 'Do Right to Me Baby (Do Unto Others)' / 'When You Gonna Wake Up' / 'Man Gave Names to All the Animals' / 'When He Returns'.

Lyrics of social criticism and spiritual anguish acutely reflected by the guitar playing of Mark Knopfler. Dylan's first Christian album is a platinum best-seller that 'spread panic.... and defections among those who wanted Dylan to sing about *their* favourite subjects' (*Guardian*).

(November–December) The first of a series of North American tours lasting until May 1980 which are defined by Dylan's refusal to sing other than his most recent Christian material. *Newsweek* characterized the early impact of Dylan's latest development: 'First came the catcalls, then ... boos. Some fans walked out; most sat through the two-hour show in stunned silence.... Dylan still looks much like the troubadour of old – black leather jacket ... and customary scowl. But ... he. ... often couldn't fill even small halls on his recent Western tour –

Appendix

and 500... marched out during the intermission in San Diego....'

1980 (January–February) North American tour.

(February) Dylan wins Grammy Award for the song 'Gotta Serve Somebody'.

(April–May) North American tour.

(June) *Saved*. Most disparaged of Dylan's Christian records ('dreadful hollowness.... vapid evasions', *London Review of Books*). Christopher Ricks discusses an example of the work on the album, the lyric 'What Can I Do for You?': 'From the beginning of the song, we are implicated in Dylan's yearning for the matching reciprocity of an answer, for a true fit; and continually the song has the honesty to deny us this.'[25]

(November–December) North American tour. Dylan introduces a set that mixes older works with Christian songs, a principle that will be followed again in the European and North American tours of 1981.

1981 (June–July) European tour. 'Astonishingly, [Dylan] was actually slow hand-clapped during a beautiful rendition of "Abraham, Martin and John". But not allowing himself to become a prisoner of his audience's expectations and still be able to sell out six nights at Earl's court and receive two standing ovations, has always been Dylan's particular talent' (*Guardian*).

(August) *Shot of Love*

'Shot of Love' / *'Heart of Mine' / 'Property of Jesus' / 'Lenny Bruce' / 'Watered-Down Love' / 'Dead Man, Dead Man' / 'In the Summertime' / 'Trouble' / 'Every Grain of Sand'.

Includes subtly cast lyrics of religious contemplation and moral urgency. Dylan observed in 1985: '*Shot of Love* didn't fit into the current formula. . . . Anyway people were always looking for some excuse to write me off and this was as good as any . . . I can't say if being "non commercial" is a put down or a compliment. . . . I think that this world is just a passing through place and that the dead have eyes and that even the unborn can see and I don't care who knows it.'[26]

(October–November) North American tour.

1982 (June) Sings at anti-nuclear rally – 'Peace Sunday' – at the Rose Bowl, Pasadena, California.

1983 (November) *Infidels*

*'Jokerman' / 'Sweetheart Like You' / 'Neighborhood Bully' / 'License to Kill' / 'Man of Peace' / 'Union Sundown' / *'I and I' / 'Don't Fall Apart on Me Tonight'.

Christian perspectives are no longer foregrounded in a collection which combines lyrics of moral valuation with two works of extreme mystical vision, 'I and I' and 'Jokerman'.

1984 (May–July) Dylan plays to three-quarters of a million on European tour with Santana. A June 'Profile' in *The Times* observed:

Dylan . . . is blowing his way up Europe from Verona to Dublin. . . . And as he duets with his old consort Joan Baez at the German dates, the response is colossal. . . .

Over the past two decades there has arisen a sort of game between Dylan and the public over 'where he's at'. The results have often proved unsatisfactory to both parties, but somehow it has acquired a dynamic of its own. Perhaps it would have been better to heed his advice, stick to the text, and leave the

Appendix

man alone. Yet because of his own elusiveness, and because of the deeply enigmatic shifts from period to period, style to style, he has connived in the process and the inquiries go on....

Why should we be thrown, after all this time, by what is only ... evidence of multiplicity? ... The only real point of surprise – and it was evident 20 years ago – is that contemporary folk music had somehow recruited a writer with serious claims to poetic excellence. Surely no one else working in the English language can have peddled popular music ... with such dense and complex lyrics. Looking back over a canon of several hundred songs, you find an astonishing breadth; sustained flights of difficult imagery, moral and religious aphorisms, metaphysical constructs, and ... crammed narratives flashing across like novels, with fugitive figures darting, like Dylan himself, in and out of the American nightmare....

The trouble was, and is, that his very presence in the rock industry has made him the butt of cultural snobbery.... Pop was meant to be an escape from reality, not an intellectual bed of nails....

(November) *Real Live*. Live performances from the 1984 tour, including a version of 'Tangled Up in Blue' with an important rewritten lyric text.

1985 (June) *Empire Burlesque*. Includes 'Tight Connection to My Heart (Has Anybody Seen My Love?)', 'When the Night Comes Falling from the Sky', 'Something's Burning, Baby'. An excursion into a highly wrought, quasi-synthesized sound, with the exception of a single acoustically performed lyric gem, 'Dark Eyes'. '[T]he themes are, well, you know, Bob Dylan themes: guilt, retribution, fear, shame, disgrace, despair, jealousy, isolation, loneliness, moral rectitude and the end of the world' (*Playboy*).

(July) Supported by Keith Richards and Ron Wood, Dylan takes part in 'Live Aid' concert (Philadelphia) for the relief of Ethiopian famine disaster, in a performance troubled by poor sound monitoring. Controversially, Dylan reminds his listeners of want at home by referring to the current American farm crisis.

(September) Performs at 'Farm Aid' concert, Champaign, Illinois.

(October) Contributes to the recording of the Artists United Against Apartheid single, 'Sun City' (released in December).

(November) *Biograph*. Warmly received retrospective collection of fifty-three pieces, presenting the spectrum of different types and registers of Dylan song up to 1981. '*Biograph*', *Time* magazine wrote, 'is a heady reminder of [Dylan's] importance': 'it is 22 years since "Blowin' in the Wind" appeared ... and a flat 20 since "Like a Rolling Stone" ... kicked rock songwriting on its head.... Dylan not only lived on the margin, he was the margin. ... Precious few have ever got near him, and no one has gone beyond. ... [T]he controversial and sometimes reviled religious rock that Dylan produced between the end of the '70's and the start of the '80's ... seems even more powerful. He started out sounding like a beat incarnation of the blues singer Blind Blake and ended sounding like a juke-joint William Blake, singing of spirits, angels, doom and deliverance.' *Biograph* offers a small but valuable selection from the body of outstanding Dylan songs never officially released, including 'Up to Me' (1974), 'Abandoned Love' (1975), and 'Caribbean Wind' (1980). In *Time* magazine Dylan observed: 'This five-record set could have been all unreleased songs. If it was worth my while, I

Appendix

could put together a ten-record set of unreleased songs, songs that have never gotten out and songs that have been bootlegged.'[27] *Biograph* also offers a small selection from the wealth of important live performances never officially released, including 'Visions of Johanna' (London, 1966), 'It's All Over Now, Baby Blue' (Manchester, 1966), and 'Isis' (Ottawa, 1975). *Biograph* became the second box-set (along with an Elvis Presley collection) to enter the top 50 of America's national Billboard charts.

Bob Dylan: Lyrics, 1962-1985, superseding the 1973 *Writings and Drawings*, published this year in the United States.

1986 (February–March) Australasian and Japanese leg of 'True Confessions' tour with Tom Petty and the Heartbreakers. A television film of a Sydney concert in February will be shown in the United States in June (subsequently released as 'Hard to Handle' videocassette).

(March) Dylan receives Founder's Award of the American Society of Composers, Authors and Publishers (ASCAP).

(June) Takes part, with Tom Petty and the Heartbreakers, in Amnesty International 'Conspiracy of Hope' concert at the Los Angeles Inglewood Forum.

(July) *Knocked Out Loaded*. Assemblage of minor songs (not all Dylan compositions), apart from one exceptional work, the eleven-minute *'Brownsville Girl'.

(June–August) 'True Confessions' tour plays to audiences of one million in North America.

(August–September) Dylan takes part, playing the role of a retired rock-singer, in the filming of *Hearts of Fire*, directed by Richard Marquand. The film will open to generally negative reviews in October 1987. '*Hearts of Fire* is hopelessly misconceived. The music is awful, the characterization facile. ... Dylan shuffles through the whole thing, clearly bemused and increasingly embarrassed' (*Melody Maker*).

1987 (September–October) European tour with Tom Petty and the Heartbreakers, closing with concerts in Britain:

The dimming of the lights ... heralded the arrival of the Zim, and provoked an instant standing ovation. ... nobody can accuse Dylan of copying his peers and merely trading on nostalgia, or buying in pre-packaged slickness. He still looks as nervous as a cat, shifting awkwardly at the microphone and jamming new chords and melodies into his songs as if he's just thought of them. The results are sometimes downright ugly, but Dylan keeps the Heartbreakers in perpetual uncertainty. ... It'll probably be different every night, in marked contrast to most artist's concerts. This is a brave, frequently exciting experiment, and the electricity is tangible. (*Guardian*)

He did not disappoint at his first Wembley concert ... being as perverse as any Jesuit priest. His determination to please himself rather than the packed arena was quite wonderful. ... you realize that you either have to swallow his genius whole or make carping criticisms. ... it is actually a relief that he does not try to talk to the audience. Enough of the feeling that lies behind [his] songs ... came across to make this the most hypnotic rock concert of the year. (*Financial Times*)

Outside the songs, he didn't speak one word – and this to a crowd hanging on his lips. ... Though he stood square on to the audience and hurled the words out. ... you were just a witness to something happening: Dylan doing his songs. ... No concessions; none needed. ... the set itself and the brief encore ended, in case anyone was still resisting 'religious Dylan', with monumental ... renditions of 'Solid Rock' and 'In the Garden'. Then he was off again without a word – without any other words. (*Sunday Telegraph*)

Appendix

1988 (January) Dylan inducted into the Rock and Roll Hall of Fame at its second annual ceremony in New York.

(May) *Down in the Groove*. Compilation mainly comprising cover versions of songs ranging from the traditional 'Shenandoah' to Blair and Robertson's 'Ninety miles an Hour (Down a Dead End Street)'. 'Lacks... that quality of dementia and incomprehensibility that makes even *Self-Portrait* a focal point in the Dylan canon' (*Spin*); 'confusing, frustrating.... *Down in the Groove* certainly makes you wonder where the middle age Dylan is bound; he still knows how to keep us guessing' (*Rolling Stone*).

(June–October) Dylan mounts much celebrated North American tour, fronting his smallest band (G. E. Smith on guitar, Christopher Parker on drums, Kenny Aaronson on bass) for twenty-three years. 'Dylan was hot in more ways than one. This was a concert of ... remarkable musicianship. ... Of all the Dylan incarnations in the past 10 to 15 years, this current trio travelling with him is providing the most punkish backup – sophisticated, polished punk, certainly, but basic... clever, always dynamic' (*Ottawa Citizen*); 'Dylan opened the show with a barrage of mid-'60s songs that were sung and played with such blistering fury that he didn't even seem to pause for a breath for the first half hour' (*Los Angeles Times*); 'Last night at New York's Radio City Music Hall, "the showplace of the nation", Dylan completed a remarkable four-night run of concerts.... an old power Dylan has rediscovered within himself, as his fiery emphasis on pre-electric material shows' (*Independent*).

(August) *Folkways. A Vision Shared: A Tribute to Woody Guthrie and Leadbelly*. Dylan sings Guthrie's 'Pretty Boy

Floyd' on this album, issued to raise funds towards the purchase by the Smithsonian Institution, Washington, of the holdings of Folkways Records and the Woody Guthrie Archive.

(October) *The Traveling Wilburys, Volume 1*. A highly successful commercial album, the result of a good-humoured collaboration between Dylan ('Lucky' Wilbury), George Harrison, Roy Orbison, Tom Petty and Jeff Lynne. It includes one specially disturbing piece, 'Tweeter and the Monkey Man', a Dylan narrative dealing, among other things, with transvestism, corruption and despair. 'This is the best record of its kind ever made. Then again, it's also the *only* record of its kind ever made. ... as on his recent stripped-down tour, Dylan sounds extraordinary, singing with the expert phrasing and wit of his best work' (*Rolling Stone*).

(December) Dylan takes part, along with Neil Young and Tracy Chapman, in a benefit concert for the Bridge School for handicapped children at the Oakland Coliseum, California.

1989 (February) *Dylan and the Dead*. Live performances from a short series of concerts undertaken with The Grateful Dead in July 1987. 'Its been a long time coming... Dylan finally teaming up with the Dead. Another artist who's determinedly gone his own hard way without a thought for public approval. ... Many cried Judas once more when Dylan last came over here, shocked by the offhand, often comic renditions of his most precious songs. These are the ... people who will find *Dylan and the Dead* sacrilegious, unable to grasp that, in the Dead, Dylan has found the perfect accomplices to keep the songs *alive*, works in progress...' (*Melody Maker*).

Appendix

(March–April) Dylan records new studio album (for release in late 1989) in New Orleans, with producer Daniel Lanois and local musicians, including the rhythm section of The Neville Brothers – Willie Green (drums), Tony Hall (bass), Brian Stolz (guitar).

(May–June) Dylan continues his gruelling schedule of concert tours since 1986 with a world tour opening in Europe (to be followed in July and August by a North American leg). In Europe Dylan once more fronts the band (Smith, Parker and Aaronson) which had accompanied him on the June–October 1988 North American tour. The mixed electric and acoustic concerts – still concentrating on 1960s material – are again marked by the peculiar force which had characterized the previous summer's tour. Reaction in the British press is enthusiastic:

The year has been crammed with ageing stars singing their past. ... But the appearance of the most powerful icon of them all is a different proposition because no-one could predict what he might do on the night. ... What we got was the happy shock of Dylan not only playing the best of his extraordinary song book but playing it with the glorious intensity of his star-burning ruthless youth. ... the voice was utterly compelling ... the quality of the songs was proven again and again. ... Dylan is still alarming ... we were faced with this extraordinary vision of a withered priest somehow plugging himself back into his unique, mystic juke box of hits. (*Guardian*)

With a fast punked-up version of 'Subterranean Homesick Blues' [Dylan] had everyone on their feet. ... 'Stuck Inside of Mobile with the Memphis Blues Again' was hammered out at a pace younger stadium-rockers would find it difficult to match. ... Propelled by some slicing work from his band, the juggernaut rolled on. A thoroughly contemporary hard rock 'All Along the Watchtower' banished memories of Jimi Hendrix. Even pared down to one voice and two acoustic guitars the flow of energy was unabated.... Fittingly, during 'I Shall Be Released' everyone went to stand down the front... 'Like a Rolling Stone' was awesome.... It was an experience much more intense than I had bargained for. (*Glasgow Herald*)

Arriving on stage with the minimum of fuss, [Dylan] tore straight into 'Subterranean Homesick Blues' at the sort of volume that would get an airport closed down.... Then the storm abated. Dylan and Smith strapped on acoustic guitars... and paced each other through an eccentric out-of-tempo version of the traditional ballad 'Barbara Allen', a practically perfect treatment of 'Girl of the North Country'.... A return to the full electric band brought... a tumultuous rendering of 'Like A Rolling Stone'.... The encores opened with another batch of acoustic songs, including a wonderfully poised 'One Too Many Mornings'.... 'Maggie's Farm' ended the concert as it had begun, with the howling electric rock-blues of the rowdiest band he has employed since the outfit that scandalized the Newport Folk Festival one historic afternoon in 1965. (*Times*)

Dylan fiercely performs songs from earlier in his career.... He does not once speak to us, only sings at us; the prime 'message' is conveyed by the finale, marking a decade of Mrs Thatcher: 'I ain't gonna work on Maggie's farm no more'.... The huge audience seems happy ... to welcome the old standards. (*London Review of Books*)

'You don't need a weather man/To know which way the wind blows', sneered Dylan, spitting out the verses like so many discarded machine-gun shells.... The '89 Zimmerman blows the cobwebs away with a fury ... he comes roaring off the blocks ... propelled by a sonic intensity that puts most garage acts back in the bedroom. (*London Evening Standard*)

Appendix

> The old master of disguise's latest manifestation is a blindingly simple success. ... he has recruited three fast-shooting sidemen ... a prolonged spell on the road has brought everything to boiling point and the result was a thrilling 75-minute show of electric blues and folk. ... [Dylan] stormed through 'Like a Rolling Stone' with magisterial authority. ... The rapturous cheers of recognition have never seemed more appropriate. (*Sunday Times*)

> In the era of Old Men And Electric Guitars ... Dylan rises supreme, mining the sonic alchemy of his mid-'60s period – the greatest, most inventive white rock 'n' roll ever recorded – to fuel an overhaul of his very own rebellious jukebox. ... Dylan reasserting himself as the rock 'n' roll vocalist par excellence. ... The meaning of the songs wasn't simply buried in nostalgia or in the lyrics, it was in the way he played with inflections and the sounds of words, the way he changes the timbre of his voice to exact the most from the frazzling guitar cauldron or the weird ... acoustic interludes. The velocity of the music makes it seem like Dylan's discovered punk and hardcore years after everyone else. But as anyone who has listened will know, he prefigured such rampages and much else back in the mercurial mid-'60s. ... His singing has never been better than on the snarling whiplash version of 'Like a Rolling Stone'. ... Dylan in '89 is living up to Neil Young's line about it being better to burn out than to fade away ... on form he is still unimpeachable, miles ahead of pretenders both young and old. (*New Musical Express*)

> Last time Dylan played the Arena, he stalked onstage looking like a commanchero scalphunter, out for blood. It was a famously confrontational performance. ... Last Thursday's concert was something else again ... the songs weren't *disfigured* by his calamitous urgency, they were given a breathless new life. ... It was not so much that these songs had been rehabilitated as almost totally *reinvented*. ... 'All Along the Watchtower' was furious, incendiary. ... 'Memphis Blues

Again' was raw, livid and loud, Dylan grinning madly as the song just took off ... delirious and deranged. ... By contrast ... 'Boots of Spanish Leather' was given an exquisitely tender reading that stunned the Wembley crowd into silence. ... The first encore ... revived the beautiful 'One Too Many Mornings', Dylan's voice a rasping ghost. ... 'Knockin' on Heaven's Door' ... went from a hushed acoustic hymn to a ferocious howling ... that took the performance ... into the blistering pandemonium of 'Maggie's Farm' which rattled Wembley to its foundations. ... this was a rejuvenated Dylan, the master in all his raging glory. (*Melody Maker*)

Notes

Chapter 1 Words

1 Interview with Jonathan Cott, *Rolling Stone*, 26 January 1978, p. 40.
2 *All What Jazz* (Faber, rev. edn., 1985), p. 151.
3 'Arnaut Daniel', *Literary Essays of Ezra Pound*, ed. T. S. Eliot (Faber, 1957; pbk. edn., 1985), pp. 116, 113.
4 Ibid., p. 112.
5 Ibid., p. 112.
6 'Bob Dylan: The Metaphor at the End of the Funnel', *Esquire*, 77 (1972), p. 188.
7 *The Force of Poetry* (Clarendon, 1984), p. 367.
8 Ibid., pp. 365–6.

Chapter 2 Mouths

1 '4 Outlined Epitaphs' are printed on the sleeve to *The Times They Are A-Changin'*. These are reprinted, with seven others, in *Lyrics, 1962-1985*. The epigraph is from the tenth in the series.
2 Reprinted as '*Highway 61 Revisited* (liner notes)' in *Lyrics, 1962-1985*.
3 Geek: 'a performer of grotesque or depraved acts in a carnival, etc.' (*Webster's Dictionary*).
4 *Rabelais and His World*, trans. Helene Iswolsky (Indiana University Press, 1984), pp. 11–12.
5 Ibid., p. 11.

6 *Revolution in Poetic Language*, trans. Margaret Waller (Columbia University Press, 1984), p. 16.
7 Ibid., p. 29.
8 Ibid., p. 29.
9 Ibid., p. 30.

Chapter 3   Reels of Rhyme

1 Interview with Cameron Crowe, included in the lyric notes to *Biograph* (as distinct from those parts of the interview included in the booklet accompanying *Biograph*).
2 Steven Goldberg, 'Bob Dylan and the Poetry of Salvation', *Bob Dylan: A Restrospective*, ed. Craig McGregor (Angus and Robertson, rev. edn., 1980), p. 186.
3 *New Society*, 4 June 1970, p. 968.
4 Alfred, Lord Tennyson, *In Memoriam*, xcv.

Chapter 4   Lady Language Creator

1 'Isis' is a joint composition by Dylan and Jacques Levy (erstwhile director of *Oh! Calcutta!*). In his notes to the lyrics on *Desire*, printed on the inner sleeve of the record, Allen Ginsberg relates of Dylan's composition of the *Desire* lyrics that 'Half-month was spent ... on Long Island with ... Jacques Levy ... sharing information.'
2 For a conflation of the various attributes of the number five, see Ad de Vries, *Dictionary of Symbols and Imagery* (North-Holland Publishing Company, rev. edn., 1976).
3 The Montreal performance of 'Isis' is released on *Biograph*. Ginsberg's note appears on the inner sleeve of *Desire*.
4 While, in live performance, Dylan will frequently and sometimes extensively alter the words of a lyric from the version given on an officially released studio album, the texts of *Lyrics, 1962–1985* for the most part conform to versions of lyrics as included on original

Notes

studio albums. In some cases, however, this general rule does not apply and the twelfth stanza of 'Isis' is an instance where the *Lyrics, 1962-1985* text has been slightly revised from that of the version performed on *Desire*.

5 *The Beckett Trilogy* (Picador, 1979), p. 355.
6 Footage of the performance comprises one of the concert sequences in *Renaldo and Clara*.
7 *Shelley's Major Poetry: The Fabric of a Vision* (Princeton University Press, 1948), p. 54.
8 Dylan's comment appears in the lyric notes to *Biograph*.
9 This version was issued on the promotional edition of *Blood on the Tracks*, November 1974.
10 This version appears as a concert sequence in *Renaldo and Clara*.
11 Lyric notes to *Biograph*.
12 Interview with Matt Damsker, 15 September 1978, *Talkin' Bob Dylan... (1978)* (Pink Elephant Productions, 1984), p. 10.
13 Interview with Jonathan Cott, *Rolling Stone*, 26 January 1978, p. 44.
14 Introduction to Part I, *Dante and his Circle*, ed. D. G. Rossetti (Ellis and White, 1874), p. 1.
15 This performance of 'Tangled Up in Blue' is released on *Real Live*. My text for the words of this version is that printed in *The Telegraph* (the journal of Wanted Man/The Bob Dylan Information Office, PO Box 22, Romford, Essex RM1 2RF, England), 21, Autumn 1985, pp. 75-6.
16 Interview with Jonathan Cott, *Rolling Stone*, 26 January 1978, p. 42.
17 St Paul, Galatians 3:28.
18 Kristeva, *Revolution in Poetic Language*, p. 29.

Chapter 5   That Enemy Within

1 The text of this lyric is taken from the *Knocked Out Loaded* songbook (Warner Brothers Publications, 1986).
2 The film alluded to is *The Gunfighter* (1950), directed by Henry King.
3 The description is Sam Shepard's, interviewed on his co-operation

with Dylan in the composition of 'Brownsville Girl' (*Rolling Stone*, 18 December 1986, p. 198).
4 May Sinclair, 'The Novels of Dorothy Richardson', *The Egoist*, 5 (April 1918), p. 58.
5 *Night of the Living Dead* (1968), directed by George A. Romero; *The Return of the Living Dead* (1985), directed by Dan O'Bannon.
6 Luke 10: 30.
7 Michael Gray, *Song and Dance Man: The Art of Bob Dylan* (Hamlyn, 2nd edn., 1981), p. 140.
8 Ibid., p. 140.
9 Dylan uses the Black American English sense of 'bad' as 'good' in the 1981 *Shot of Love* lyric 'Lenny Bruce': 'Lenny Bruce was bad, he was the brother that you never had.'
10 Matthew 21: 12.

Chapter 6 To Separate the Good from the Bad

1 H. J. C. Grierson, ed., *The Poems of John Donne*, 2 vols. (Oxford University Press, 1912), vol. ii, p. 241.
2 A performance of this lyric, not included on any Dylan album, was released as a record single together with 'Gotta Serve Somebody' in September 1979.

Chapter 7 That Forbidden Zone

1 'Second manifeste du surréalisme' [1929], *Les Manifestes du surréalisme* (Editions du Sagittaire, 1946), p. 111.
2 Transcribed from unofficial concert recording.
3 Of the lyrics mentioned below that are associated with the *Blonde on Blonde* recording sessions, performances of neither 'She's Your Lover Now' (1965) nor 'I Wanna Be Your Lover' (1965) were released on *Blonde on Blonde*, but a performance of 'I Wanna Be Your Lover' is included on *Biograph*.
4 cf. chapter 4, n. 13.

Notes

5 *Voice Without Restraint: Bob Dylan's Lyrics and their Background* (Paul Harris, 1981), p. 29.
6 'Le Mystère dans les lettres', *Œuvres Complètes* (Gallimard, 1945), p. 387.
7 *The Idea of the Holy* (Oxford University Press, 1923; pbk. edn., 1970), p. 19.
8 Interview with Scott Cohen, *Spin*, December 1985, p. 39.
9 The prophecy in Isaiah 21:1-10 apparently alludes to an earlier siege of Babylon than the one at the close of the Israelite exile.
10 The emblem of the hand grasping a snake or eel goes back to Genesis 9:2 ('The fear of you and the dread of you shall be ... upon all that moveth upon the earth, and upon all the fishes of the sea; into your hand are they delivered'). One of the principal significations of the emblem is the magistrate's control of wrongdoing – the leader's responsibility. A well-known instance of the emblem is Andrea Alciati's IN DEPREHENSUM; cf. Emblem 21 in *Andreas Alciatus. Index Emblematicus*, vol. I: *The Latin Emblems*, ed. Peter M. Daly, Virginia W. Callahan, Simon Cuttler (University of Toronto Press, 1985).
11 The 'certain rich man' of Luke 16:19-31 is unnamed and thus conveniently referred to as 'Dives'.
12 *A Dictionary of Symbols* (English trans., Routledge and Kegan Paul, pbk. edn., 1981), pp. 110-11.
13 Elements in the icon of the woman and the prince in this stanza, with its tonalities of an anti-Christ, recall the figure of the enemy of the people of God – the antithesis of 'the bride', the 'new Jerusalem' – in Revelation 17:3-5: 'I saw a woman sit upon a scarlet coloured beast .../And the woman was arrayed in purple and scarlet colour .../And upon her forehead was a name written, MYSTERY, BABYLON THE GREAT, THE MOTHER OF HARLOTS AND ABOMINATIONS OF THE EARTH'.
14 For the bird as a symbol of the soul and for a conflation of the multiple and contradictory attributes of both nightingale and moon, see de Vries, *Dictionary of Symbols and Imagery*.
15 Milton, *Paradise Lost*, ix, 121-2.

Notes

16 Dylan: 'What hangs everybody up is that I'm not *stopping*', *Time Out*, 16-22 June 1978, p. 10.

Appendix   Chronology of Dylan's Career and Officially Released Recordings

1 Interview with Cameron Crowe, *Biograph* booklet, p. 5.
2 Ed Ward, Geoffrey Stokes and Ken Tucker, *Rock of Ages. The 'Rolling Stone' History of Rock and Roll* (Summit Books, 1986; Penguin, 1987), p. 256.
3 Interview with Nat Hentoff, *New Yorker* (October 1964); reprinted in McGregor, *Bob Dylan: A Retrospective*, p. 29.
4 Ibid., p. 19.
5 Ward, Stokes and Tucker, *Rock of Ages*, p. 306.
6 Brock Helander, *The Rock Who's Who* (Schirmer Books, 1982), p. 146.
7 Ibid., p. 147.
8 Ward, Stokes and Tucker *Rock of Ages*, pp. 310-11.
9 *Contemporary Literary Criticism*, 23 vols. (Gale, 1973-84), vol. iii, p. 130.
10 Ward, Stokes and Tucker, *Rock of Ages*, pp. 303, 311-12, 314.
11 Ibid., p. 309.
12 Helander, *The Rock Who's Who*, p. 149.
13 *Playboy* interview (March 1966); reprinted in McGregor, *Bob Dylan: A Retrospective* pp. 61-2.
14 Cited in *Biograph* booklet, p. 12.
15 Ibid., p. 15.
16 Helander, *The Rock Who's Who*, p. 147.
17 For lists of known lyrics not included in *Lyrics, 1962-1985*, see Clinton Heylin, '*Lyrics, 1962-1985*: A Collection Short of the Definitive', in Michael Gray and John Bauldie, eds., *All Across The Telegraph: A Bob Dylan Handbook* (Sidgwick and Jackson, 1987), pp. 229-42.
18 Ward, Stokes and Tucker, *Rock of Ages*, p. 389.
19 Kermode 'Bob Dylan', p. 188.

Notes

20 Ibid., p. 110.
21 Jacques Levy, cited in John Bauldie, 'Jacques Levy and the *Desire* Collaboration', in Gray and Bauldie, *All Across The Telegraph*, p. 160.
22 Cited in Robert Shelton, *No Direction Home: The Life and Music of Bob Dylan* (New English Library, 1986), p. 454.
23 *The Rolling Thunder Logbook* (Penguin, 1978), p. 43.
24 Cited by John Bauldie and Michael Gray, 'Interviews and a Poem: Allen Ginsberg, Poet', in Gray and Bauldie, *All Across The Telegraph*, p. 165.
25 Christopher Ricks, 'What He Can Do For You', in Gray and Bauldie, *All Across The Telegraph*, p. 188.
26 *Biograph* booklet, pp. 24, 31.
27 Interview with Denise Worrell, *Time*, 25 November 1985, p. 53.

Index

'Abandoned Love', 22
'Abraham, Martin and John', 168
absolute, the, 129–30
absurd, the, 16
'Alastor' (Shelley), 48
alienation (*see also under* self; soul), 11, 66–9, 84
Alk, Howard, 156
'All Along the Watchtower', 132–3
American dream, the, 75
anima, 38, 91, 93, 107, 124
Another Side of Bob Dylan (album), 149
artistic creation (*see also* imagination), 19–35
    cycle of, 26–32
    preparation for, 23–4, 38
    and self, 6, 32–5

Baez, Joan, 148, 169
Babylon, fall of, 132–3
Baker, Carlos, 48
Bakhtin, Mikhail, 14
'Ballad of a Thin Man', 10–17
Ballantine, Christopher, 28
Band, The, 155, 160, 162
Basement Tapes, The (album), 156–7, 162
Beauty, 68–9
Beckett, Samuel, 46
Before the Flood (album), 161

Belafonte, Harry, 146
Biograph (album), 171
blindman's buff, 116
Blood on the Tracks (album), 161–2
Bloom, Allan, 151
Bloomfield, Mike, 154
Blonde on Blonde (album), 111–12, 156
'Blowin' in the Wind', 142, 147
Bob Dylan (album), 147
Bob Dylan at Budokan (album), 167
Bob Dylan's Greatest Hits (album), 156
Bob Dylan's Greatest Hits Vol. 2 (album), 159
Breton, André, 110
Bringing It All Back Home (album), 28, 149–51
Brooks, Harvey, 153
Browning, Robert, 36
'Brownsville Girl', 71–9
Butterfield, Paul, 152
'Byzantium' (Yeats), 21

'Caribbean Wind', 71
carnival images, use of, 14–15, 17, 21, 80–1, 84, 88
Carter, Rubin, 163–4
'Changing of the Guards', 96
Christ, 95, 107, 108, 134, 139
Christian love, 102–3, 105

Index

Christian lyrics, 7, 95–109, 167–9
Cirlot, J. E., 139
cliché, use of, 4–5, 46, 72, 76
Concert for Bangladesh (album and film), 159
creative processes, *see* artistic creation
culture, *see* Western culture

Dante Alighieri, 62
'Dead Man, Dead Man', 100–1, 105
death, 46, 99, 134, 137
    and rebirth, 40–2, 127–8
    spiritual, 105–6
Desire (album), 164
    sleeve notes (Ginsberg), 36, 181
desire, 38, 42, 47
desires and drives, overwhelming reason, 36, 48
'Desolation Row', 81–91
Dionysius the Areopagite, 110
division, and reunification, 37–8, 40–1
Don't Look Back (film), 151
Down in the Groove (album), 174
dreams, 126
drives, *see* desires and drives
Duchamp, Marcel, 116
Dylan (album), 160
Dylan, Bob
    on *Biograph*, 171
    on *Blood on the Tracks*, 61
    Christianity of, *see* Christian lyrics
    concerts and tours by, 145–79
    on early influences, 145
    electrified instruments, use of, 152–3
    on 'eye', 8–9
    on 'I', 131
    love lyrics of, *see* love
    on 'Mr. Tambourine Man', 19
    muse of, 20, 28
    narrative, use of, *see* narrative structure

    persona, transformations of, 2
    pronouns, use of, *see* pronouns
    on *Renaldo and Clara*, 1
    on rock and roll, 154
    on *Shot of Love*, 169
    on 'Tangled Up in Blue', 58, 61
    on time, 61, 118
    on Tom Paine Award, 148

Dylan and the Dead (album), 175

Eat the Document (film), 155–6
Eckhart, Meister, 110
Ecclesiastes (Bible), 124, 134
Ed Sullivan Show, 148
'11 Outlined Epitaphs', 8
Eliot, T. S., 89
Elizabethans, the, 3
Empire Burlesque (album), 170
'Epipsychidion' (Shelley), 48
'Eternal Circle', 18, 28–32, 34
'Every Grain of Sand', 100–1
evil, 105, 108
'eye', pun on 'I', 8–9
Exodus (Bible), 125

faith, 97
female figures,
    as archetype, 63
    as inspiration, 28–32
    stereotypes of, 121
fertility myths, 40
fiction and reality, blurring of, 74, 76–7
five, 37
flowers, 33
Folkways. A Vision Shared: A Tribute to Woody Guthrie and Leadbelly (album), 174–5
Fool, the, 139
freedom, and 'boundaries of rhyme', 22
Freewheelin' Bob Dylan, The (album), 148

Index

Gehenna, 124
Genesis (Bible), 184
Ginsberg, Allen, 36, 42, 165, 181
God, 98, 125, 130-1
'Golden Loom', 19
'Gonna Change My Way of Thinking', 98-9, 108
'Gotta Serve Somebody', 98
Grateful Dead, 175
Great Goddess, 37
Guthrie, Woody, 96, 146, 174-5

Hard Rain (album and film), 164
'Hard Rain's A-Gonna Fall, A', 90, 147
Hard to Handle (video film), 172
Harrison, George, 159, 175
heart, the, *see* love
'Heart of Mine', 103-5
Hearts of Fire (film), 172
Helm, Levon, 153
Herdman, John, 120
Highway 61 Revisited (album), 2, 9, 153-4
  sleeve notes (Dylan), 8
Hooker, John Lee, 146

I, *see* self
'I', in lyrics
  becoming 'he', 50, 57-8, 65
  becoming 'she', 65
'I and I', 1, 124-31
'I Shall Be Free No. 10', 149
'I Shall Be Released', 49-51
'I Wanna Be Your Lover', 112
identity, *see* self
'Idiot Wind', 161
'If Dogs Run Free', 159
imagination (*see also* artistic creation)
  as anima, 91
  autonomy of, 91-2
  dark side of, 105-9

divided from conscious self, 12-13, 92, 126
gender of, 65
and language, 16-17, 25
and reason, 17
and unconscious self, 20
imago, 44
In Memoriam (Tennyson), 80
Infidels (album), 169
inspiration, 19-20, 25-6, 35
  as female figure, 28-32
Isaiah (Bible), 130, 132-3
'Isis', 36-48, 66, 68, 81
  Montreal version, live 4/12/75, 42, 48
'It's All Over Now, Baby Blue', 79-81

Jester, the, 138-9
John Wesley Harding (album), 157
Joker, the, 139
'Jokerman', 9, 131-43

Kermode, Frank, 4, 158, 159
King, Martin Luther, Jr., 148
Knocked Out Loaded (album), 77, 172
Knopfler, Mark, 167
knowledge, 10-11
Kooper, Al, 153, 154
Kristeva, Julia, 16

Langhorne, Bruce, 150
language
  and imagination, 16-17, 25
  of love, *see under* love
  and self, *see under* self, conscious; self, unconscious
  surrealist, *see* surrealist language
Larkin, Philip, 2
Last Waltz, The (album and film), 164-5
'Lay, Lady, Lay', 158
'Lenny Bruce', 183

Index

Leviticus (Bible), 125
Levy, Jacques, 181
'Life in a Love' (Browning), 36
'Like a Rolling Stone', 9, 81, 151
LHOOQ (Duchamp), 116
Live Aid, 171
'Lonesome Death of Hattie Carroll', 148
love, 28, 32-4, 103-5, 119
    Christian, *see* Christian love
    language of, 48
    rhetoric of, 23
'Love Minus Zero/No Limit', 18, 32-5
Luke (Bible), 138
lyrics
    compared to poetry, 2-3
    performance of, 2, 5
Lyrics 1962-1985 (Dylan), 172

Mallarmé, Stephane, 17, 122
'Man of Peace', 140
Marquand, Richard, 172
marriage, 37-8, 40-1, 43, 45
Masterpieces (album), 166
materialism, 47
Matthew (Bible), 134
May, 37
meaning, audience participation in, 2, 60
memory, 72-5
'memory and fate', repression of, 21-3
mind, *see* self, conscious; self, unconscious
'Mister Jones', *see* 'Ballad of a Thin Man'
'Mr. Tambourine Man', 18-28, 33-4, 65, 81, 149
modernist literature, 16
modernist poetry, 4, 60, 91
Mona Lisa, 115-16
'mouths', of the self, 8-9

Muses, 20
'My Back Pages', 79
Mystical Theology, The (Dionysius), 110

narrative structure, fragmentation of
    in 'Brownsville Girl', 72-3
    in 'Shelter From the Storm', 67
    in 'Tangled Up in Blue', 52, 57-61, 64
    in 'Visions of Johanna', 112, 117-18
Nashville Skyline (album), 157-8
Neville Brothers, 176
New Morning (album), 159
'New Pony', 93-5
Newport Folk Festival 1965, 151-2
'Obviously Five Believers', 111
'One of Us Must Know (Sooner or Later)', 111
Other, the, 43, 47, 110, 117, 130
Otto, Rudolf, 130

Pat Garrett and Billy the Kid (album and film), 160
Paul, Saint, 139-40
Peck, Gregory, 72, 74-5, 78
Peckinpah, Sam, 159
Pennebaker, D. A., 151
personality, *see* self
Petty, Tom, and the Heartbreakers, 172, 173
poetic creation, *see* artistic creation
Pound, Ezra, 3
'Precious Angel', 98, 106-8
pronouns, play of
    in 'I Shall Be Released', 50-1
    in 'Isis', 44
    in 'Tangled Up in Blue', 51-2, 65
    in 'Visions of Johanna', 116-17
'Property of Jesus', 97
Provençals, the, 3
Psyche, *see* self; soul

quest narratives, 40

Index

rational, the (*see also* reason), 12–13, 15–16
rationalism, 11–12
  surrealist subversion of, 13, 17
Real Live (album), 170
reality and fiction, blurring of, 74, 76–7
reason (*see also* rational, the)
  and imagination, 17
  overwhelmed by desires and drives, 36, 48
rebirth, 40–2, 127–8
refrains, in lyrics, 5
regeneration myths, 40
Renaldo and Clara (film), 1, 165–6
reunification, 37–8, 40–1
reunion, 42–4
Revelation (Bible), 184
Richards, Keith, 171
Ricks, Christopher, 4–5, 168
Rimbaud, Arthur, 'I is another', 50
Rivera, Scarlet, 164
Robertson, Robbie, 153, 155
Rolling Thunder Revue, 162–5
Rossetti, Dante Gabriel, 62

Santana, 169
Scorsese, Martin, 165
Seeger, Pete, 152
self
  and the absolute, 129–30
  alienation from, 42, 119–20, 126–7
  as 'becoming', 47
  conscious
    divided from imagination, 12–13, 92, 126
    divided from soul, 64, 129
    divided from unconscious, 8–9, 13, 42–4
    integrated with unconscious, 26, 37–8, 42
    as language, 43, 46–7
    in language, 6–7, 13, 43–4, 46–8
    in time, 21–3, 60–1, 64, 119, 143
  creative, *see* artistic creation; imagination
  as culturally defined, 75, 84
  dissolution of, 65
  and God, 125, 130–1
  and the heart, 103–5
  imaginative, *see* artistic creation; imagination
  as joker, 132
  as Jokerman, 133–43
  masculine side of, 38, 41
  'mouths' of, 8–9
  and Other, 43, 47, 110, 117, 130
  and others, 43–4, 66–7
  rational, *see* rational, the
  splitting into selves, 50–1, 57, 116–17, 120–1, 129, 137
  as thief, 132
  unconscious (*see also* soul)
    anima of, 38, 93, 107
    divided from conscious, 8–9, 13, 42–3
    and dream, 126
    as 'forbidden zone', 110–11, 124
    gender of, 65
    and imagination, 20
    imago of, 44
    integrated with conscious, 26, 37–8, 42
    and language, 16–17, 65
    repression of, 12
self-alienation, *see* self, alienation from
self-fulfilment, 49
Self Portrait (album), 158–9
'Senor', 95
Sermon XCIX (Eckhart), 110
'She Belongs to Me', 91–2
'She's Your Lover Now', 111
Shelley, Percy Bysshe, 48

Index

'Shelter from the Storm', 66–70
Shepard, Sam, 71, 163
'Shot of Love', 100, 102
Shot of Love (album), 96, 168–9
sleep, 126–7
'Slow Train Coming', 98–9
Slow Train Coming (album), 96, 167
Smith, G. E., 174, 176, 177
'Song to Woody', 96
soul (*see also* self, unconscious), 64–7
    ahistoricity of, 61, 118
    alienation from, 100–1
    creative, *see* artistic creation; imagination
    divided from conscious self, 64, 129
    gender of, 65
Stokes, Geoffrey, 152–3
Street Legal (album), 166
'Stuck Inside of Mobile with the Memphis Blues Again', 111–12
'Subterranean Homesick Blues', 22
'Sun City', 171
surrealist language, use of, 13, 17, 113

'Talkin' John Birch Paranoid Blues', 148
'Talkin' World War III Blues', 148
'Tambourine Man', *see* 'Mr. Tambourine Man'
'Tangled Up in Blue', 48–9
    Blood on the Tracks version, 51–66
    Boston version, live 21/11/75, 55, 63, 65
    Brussels version, live 7/6/84, 110–11
    Real Live version, live London 7/7/84, 63, 65, 110, 170
    unreleased studio version 12/9/74, 55, 57–8
Tarantula (Dylan), 159
Tarot, the, 139
'Temporary Like Achilles', 111

Tennyson, Alfred, Lord, 80, 181
time
    break up of, 27, 58, 61, 121
    and conscious self, *see under* self, conscious
    and soul, *see under* soul
    suspension of, 21–3
Times They are A-Changin', The (album), 148
Timothy (Bible), 125
'Tombstone Blues', 11–12
Traveling Wilburys, Volume 1 (album), 175
Trickster, the, 140
troubadours, 3
'Trouble', 96–7
'Trouble in Mind', 106
'Tweeter and the Monkey Man', 175

union
    of opposites, 37
    and reunion, 42–4
Unnameable, The (Beckett), 46
'Up to Me', 50

visions, *see* 'Visions of Johanna'
'Visions of Johanna', 111–24
Vita Nuova (Dante), 62

Wasteland, The (Eliot), 89
'Watered-Down Love', 105
Western culture, as waste land, 75, 82–9
Westerns, 38, 71–5
'What Can I Do For You?', 168
'When He Returns', 102
'When You Gonna Wake Up?', 47, 97–8
'Where Are You Tonight? (Journey Through Dark Heat)', 95
Wood, Ron, 171
Word, the, 25–6, 28

192

Index

words, special status of, 5
Writings and Drawings (Dylan), 160

Yeats, W. B., 21

'You're Gonna Make Me Lonesome When You Go', 23

Zimmerman, Robert Allen, *see* Dylan, Bob